The

DICTIONARY
of
CORPORATE
BULLSHIT

The
DICTIONARY
of
CORPORATE
BULLSHIT

*AN A TO Z LEXICON OF EMPTY, ENRAGING,
AND JUST PLAIN STUPID OFFICE TALK*

LOIS BECKWITH

Broadway Books
New York

BROADWAY

PRINTED IN THE UNITED STATES OF AMERICA

BROADWAY BOOKS and its logo, a letter B bisected on the
diagonal, are trademarks of Random House, Inc.

Visit our website at www.broadwaybooks.com

First edition published March 2006.

Book design by Michael Collica

Library of Congress Cataloging-in-Publication Data

Beckwith, Lois.
The dictionary of corporate bullshit : an A to Z lexicon of empty,
enraging, and just plain stupid office talk / Lois Beckwith.—1st ed.
p.   cm.
1. Business—Dictionaries.   2. Business—Terminology.
3. Office practice—Dictionaries.   I. Title.

HF1001.B43 2006
650'.03—dc22   2005050744

ISBN 0-7679-2074-0

3 5 7 9 10 8 6 4

For my parents, with endless love and thanks, who somehow managed to raise a rebellious conformist

And for the workers of the world.
We shall overcome one day.

In the confrontation between the river and the rock, the river always wins . . . not through strength but by perseverance.

—"Perseverance," Successories®

Go over, go under, go around, or go through. But never give up.

—"Never Give Up," Successories®

Introduction

Welcome home. The fact that you bought this book—for yourself, for someone you love or care about, or, for that matter, for someone you really, really hate with the proverbial intensity of a thousand hot burning suns—is a sign that you have crossed over to the land of those fed up with Corporate Bullshit. Feels so good!

The most important thing for you to know is that you are not alone. The crying jags in the bathroom; the overwhelming sense of injustice, underappreciation, frustration, and duplicity; the impulse to inflict bodily harm on an extremely annoying or undermining coworker or boss, are all deeply familiar, and, in fact, commonplace here. We all feel it. Around the country. Every day. And we're mad as hell and we're not going to take it anymore.

Much has been written about the pervasive use of corporate "buzzwords" in business and office culture. At this point, that's kind of an old story. This language was playfully lampooned through the popular "Buzzword Bingo" game of the late nineties, and most people found this talk ridiculous, bloated, or mildly annoying at worst. But people were making money then, so it was all in good fun. As you probably know: Times have changed.

Not only is corporate bullshit less amusing when paired with a "challenging" economic climate, but more people than ever before are using *more* bullshit. A fast fact: It was recently estimated that as many as four out of every five employees use buzzwords to keep up with their colleagues, without "having a clue" as to what these words mean.

All the language is still there, injected into meaningless marathon meetings, PowerPoint presentations, corporate memos, and "feedback" from your boss and "colleagues," but the fact is that corporate bullshit has taken over, tainting almost every interaction between the citizens of the business world. People have stopped communicating. They have, as you know, stopped talking to each other like normal people.

A new era of corporate bullshit is upon us, and it is far more sinister than the words some Bschool grad, crusty veteran, or dot-com kid can dole out. It goes beyond empty phrases like "at the end of the day," "a sense of urgency," and "on the same page" and corrupts words like "lunch," "celebrate," "passion," and "commitment," which take on whole new meanings in this environment.

However, the most dangerous element of corporate bullshit is outside the realm of language altogether. This sickness has placed a stranglehold on our culture of work, affecting how we relate to and treat each other. It enables incompetence, iniquity, and frankly, inhumanity. At this point, language is merely the vehicle through which the bullshit is communicated.

About ten years ago I entered the workforce like so many other recent college grads: I was "bright-eyed and bushy-tailed," I was optimistic and ambitious, I wanted to work hard and well, and find my place in the professional world. (I was also a lot thinner.)

Needless to say, I got slammed—big-time. I exerted a lot of pointless effort trying to make sense of the completely non-sensical and find logic in a world where up is down and down is up. As they say: If I only knew then what I know now.

It's too late for me, but it's probably not for so many of you. Forget *The 7 Habits of Highly Effective People.* Spend more time kissing ass, laughing disingenuously, blowing out your hair, and playing golf. And, of course, studying this book—because this is how it really works.

For those of you who find yourself with me in the great conference room, the collective "town hall" of the angry, fed up, and apathetic, I hope you'll find comfort in seeing all of this bullshit out there in the open for all to see, and know, once and for all, that you're not crazy.

They are.

Keep the faith,
Lois Beckwith

A

accounts payable 1. department responsible for processing the fulfillment of **invoices** rendered to a company **2.** one of the least glamorous and most underappreciated departments of any organization, as its staff members are seen as merely number-crunchers and paper-pushers; identified by sprawling and depressing **cube** farms, big calculators, and the palpable sense that the employees there know that no one knows their names and, really, doesn't care, and/or the thought, "I went into accounting because I thought it would grant me job security . . . but this sucks. And PS: Screw these elitist liberal arts grads hounding me for checks." **3.** may behave as policy Nazis, due to the fact that any previous deviation from departmental rules (perhaps encouraged by an **office flirt**) has resulted in serious reprimand and multiple departmental **memos 4.** a black hole for **in-**voices; when you inquire about the status of an **invoice,** you will inevitably be met with the uncaring statement that there is no record of it and it must be resubmitted, indicating the need to begin the process all over again, even though your job depends on delivering a check the next day; and, resubmitting means securing sign-off from your **boss,** who is too busy having **lunch** at a nice restaurant to approve the payment of a bill. In extreme circumstances you will have to venture to the accounts payable department to physically retrieve an unsigned **invoice,** check, etc., to ensure payment and the avoidance of the cancellation of a priority contract.

acronym 1. a term formed with some of the letters (often the initials) of a phrase, used as an abbreviation **2.** "words" that are so prevalent in business that people will often string them together with a few articles to form a complete sentence, and worse, not even realize they are doing it. The fact that people constantly ask them to translate what they have just said does not deter them from doing this. **3.** terms that are frequently indecipherable to those not "in the know" (i.e., people who speak plain English), and which therefore serve to alienate them and make them feel stupid. People may enlist the use of acronyms for this very purpose.

action items 1. issues on a **meeting** agenda that require decisions **2.** issues that are classified as such because no one wanted to deal with them/take responsibility for them in the last **meeting,** that suddenly require **vetting,** a deep dive, etc., and therefore will be tabled until the next **meeting.** *Also see* **parking lot.**

actionable 1. giving grounds for legal action **2.** that's right, this is a legal term, and doesn't actually mean "the things that can be done," as it's repeatedly hijacked by the smarty-pants who went to **Bschool 3.** the things that can actually be accomplished or **moved forward** on,

e.g., boss: "Tom, how many of the eight items in this proposal would you say are actionable in the next six months?" Tom: "Uh, maybe two."

add-value 1. to increase the worth of something by supplementing it with services, products, or access to resources **2.** classic **sales** and **marketing** speak used to justify charging more than the competitor by offering frequently intangible and often unquantifiable things like "knowledge" or "experience," which are referred to as "value adds." Employees will continually be hounded by management to find ways of adding value to products so that the company can jack up the price. **3.** means nothing in terms of quality, especially since *anything* can be claimed to add value

administrative assistant 1. junior employee who supports an executive or department through the execution of administrative tasks **2.** whatever you do, *do not* call these people secretaries, because they really don't want to be associated with those people. PS: Depending on how long they've been around or the status of the exec they support, they might make *a lot* more money than you, so when you're wondering why they have Prada boots and you shop at T.J. Maxx, now you know. **3.** employees who are highly valued for their **attention to detail,** in part because their boss claims to be focusing on the **big picture** and doesn't "do details," but in fact can't balance his own checkbook and would be rendered helpless if he had to do his administrative assistant's job; for administrative assistants who have taken a job with the hope that they can **move from within,** their rigorous **attention to detail** and achievement of **excellence** may in the end be used against them, as these qualities will not be seen as a reason to advance them to another job that challenges them; instead, they will be **pigeonholed** as a member of **support staff,** and the person they report to will fight like hell to keep them in their current position, because, you know, good help is so hard to find these days.

advocate 1. one who supports a person or issue **2.** what senior members of an organization avow they will be for a junior employee or cause, a promise they immediately forget when the opportunity to do so presents itself **3.** employees may be told they need to be an advocate for themselves, which is the **boss's** way of saying, "Although it is my job to be aware of your performance and reward you for doing good work, I'll never do that unless you tell me exactly what it is you do around here. You should not count on me to know this information, or certainly, to give you a raise or promotion unless you hound me about it."

antidepressant 1. medication used to manage depression **2.** a prescribed medicine that in the past, you never really felt a need for, but when you started having **crying** jags in your **cube,** losing your mind, and couldn't concentrate on anything, your therapist suggested you should check them out. And by God, you don't know how you would go to work every day without them! *See also* **Zoloft, Zyban.**

ASAP 1. *abbr* as soon as possible **2.** a last-minute qualifier delivered to junior employees that is always preceded by "I/we need this"; the "as possible" implies some flexibility, and a recognition that a late-breaking request may encroach on other, perhaps equally urgent matters already being attended to. However, it really means "stop everything you're doing and take care of this now. I don't care what else you have going on." **3.** often used when requesting something that the person making the demand knows full well, due to normal business hours, red tape, the sign-off of an SVP currently vacationing in Tahiti, etc., will require several days to accomplish

ass-kisser 1. a person who engages in **kissing ass.** *Also known as* a brown-noser. *See* **kissing ass.**

as you know 1. a phrase invoked to indicate that what is about to be said is information the audience is well aware of **2.** a phrase invoked to indicate that what is about to be said is information the audience is probably not at all aware of, but probably should be aware of (because it was on the front page of the *New York Times* or discussed in a high-priority memo they received the week before or was in all of the **trade publications**) but that the speaker is going to give them a pass on and tell them about so they can act like they knew

about it all along. Used in **ass-kissing** situations like **sales** presentations or any forum in which the speaker has something to gain from the people they are speaking to; otherwise, the individuals receiving the information would be quizzed on the subject in an attempt to **bust** them.

at Stanford/Wharton/Princeton/ Harvard . . . 1. a conversational reference to where the speaker went to school and its philosophy/culture; most often citing work at the graduate level **2.** sign of a major elitist tool who in reality probably isn't that smart, as he wouldn't need to mention his Ivy League credentials when recommending a good burger joint if he were; it's not enough that these people went to a premier/expensive school and may have secured an **interview** or job through a particularly rousing night of drinking scotch or by attending a delightful tea at the club, they *need to let you know.* **3.** major irony: many titans of the corporate world went to Joe Blow University and really don't give a shit where people went to school, in fact, may regard highly credentialed colleagues as nancy boys or softies. *Also see* **Bschool.**

at the end of the day 1. not the literal end of the day, as in sunset, 5:30 P.M., 7:00 P.M., etc. The end result, The final analysis, When all is said and done, When the pedal hits the metal, When the shit hits the fan, When I'm reviewing my mutual fund balances and realize my kid is going to a state school . . . A phrase uttered in conclusion by managers who are supposedly explaining a somewhat nonsensical corporate tenet/idea/policy/decision that probably does not make sense. ("At the end of the day, **it is what it is.**") A nice way to end a thought, thrown in to infuse a statement with an air of authority, common sense, and definitive finality. A common leitmotif; it just sounds good. *See also* **bottom line, net-net.**

attention to detail 1. diligent and focused concentration on the smaller components of one's job **2.** if you are a junior staffer, this will be your downfall; any mistake you make will be attributed to your *lack* of attention to detail, regardless of how many details you did pay attention to. No crises will result from your oversight, it will just be an error made, which happens to humans, who are made of flesh and blood and are fallible, unlike machines and computers— oh wait, they make errors, *too.* **3.** something everyone says they have in a job **interview;** totally meaningless claim, often untrue **4.** should your **boss** independently make a mistake that is caused by his own lack of attention to detail, it will be your fault. *Important caveat:* Do not shirk on attention to detail when ordering the **boss's** salad niçoise **lunch** or **company car** to ferry him to the airport for his vacation in Capri, as he tends to get very cranky about these mishaps above all else.

avoidance 1. the act of deliberately keeping away from someone or something **2.** essential survival skill in the corporate world **3.** physical avoidance involving strategic adjustment of commonly traveled routes, creative and sometimes inefficient use of multiple elevator banks and the connections they provide, attempts to embed oneself in a large crowd waiting for an elevator, utilization of entries and exits other than the main one (parking garage, loading dock, etc.), and sometimes just flat-out running **4.** digital avoidance can be attempted by simply not returning **e-mail** or phone messages, or using **caller**

ID to screen unwanted calls; a more conciliatory form of avoidance is to assure someone that you are "working on it," or to promise delivery at a time/date of your choosing and then not honor it.

B

bandwidth 1. resources available in the form of time, staff, etc. **2.** most frequently used in a negative context, denying its availability, e.g., "I just don't have the bandwidth right now" (It is rare to see people running around saying, "I've got all this bandwidth I'm not doing anything with—anybody got a project I can take on?"); very useful way of saying "I don't feel like doing that" without actually saying it, with the extra bonus of making it seem like you're really **swamped 3.** a claim of low bandwidth can also be used as a tactic to get more funding, staff, equipment, etc. e.g., "I don't have the bandwidth, but if you allow me to hire for the position that I've been telling you has needed to be filled for months, some bandwidth might appear." **4.** may also indicate that the people with low bandwidth don't want to work more than the two or so days per week they currently are. *See also* **push back.**

bathroom 1. the place where you go to perform essential bodily functions **2.** the first place you are shown as a new employ, by a fellow staffer who is resisting telling you all the reasons it sucks to work there **3.** for the cubicle set, the favored place for **crying** when struck by a particularly rough breakup, unfair retribution/public humiliation from the **boss**, or the overwhelming sense that your life is shit and you're never going anywhere, ever **4.** site of bizarre intragender scolding regarding hygiene [primarily female], found in the form of eight-and-one-half-by-eleven-inch sheets of paper taped to the wall castigating fellow users with statements in the spirit of "Your mother does not work here"; "Learn to love the art of flushing"; "If you sprinkle when you tinkle . . ."; and "Were you raised in a barn?!" **5.** also realm of uncomfortable monitoring/timing when it's okay to do a number two; some employees, most frequently men, will attempt to casually make their way to or from the bathroom with reading material, as if they are not announcing either "I am about to" or "I just did" take a shit; execs tend to relieve themselves with abandon, indicating their place in the social hierarchy, and may even conduct **conference calls** while on the can, an act that makes those in the bathroom uncomfortable as well as those who are subjected to the sound of flushing in the background during their **meeting. 6.** may also be the site of repeated encounters with a **weird person,** whom you get trapped in **small talk** with, or of a supreme **busting** in which you are openly bitching/**gossiping** with a coworker only to have your **boss** or another senior staffer emerge from a stall

the work of their anonymous **team;** most battery cells are aware of their plight, which causes them extreme frustration and resentment. **3.** very sci-fi; think *Coma, The Matrix,* or any cinematic portrayal of a helpless body in a pod delivering, against its will, some kind of energy or sustenance to an oppressive entity via a tube

bcc 1. *lit* blind carbon copy **2.** an option available in **e-mail** programs that allows people to "copy" others without the recipient being aware **3.** so nasty and **passive-aggressive;** essentially a way of "telling" on someone, the act of a child who can't handle things on his own **4.** can be useful for **busting** someone who is being a total jerk to you, in which case it's awesome; also a helpful way to tell your **boss,** "Um, can you step in here, because I don't have the authority to rip this person a new one. **Thanks.**"

battery cell 1. a self-contained remote source of energy **2.** a productive employee who generates ideas and, due to the nature of the reporting structure, provides them to his **boss,** who then embraces the concepts and claims them as her own, or as

beauty pageant 1. a presentation created with particular emphasis on impressing the intended audience **2.** a dog and pony show with lots of flash or impressive information created with the goal of seducing the audience and enchanting them into abandoning all critical thought; low on details, high on the inclusion of attractive execs and well-known **brands,** or, when applicable, **talent**

benefit dinner 1. a formal meal organized in the name of raising funds for a charitable cause through the purchase of place settings, usually in increments of tables **2.** hoity-toity affairs held in fancy venues that feature a cocktail hour during which everyone scarfs finger food, hits the high-shelf open bar, schmoozes, and checks each other out—particularly the wives of execs who are each, individually, wearing more sequins and showing more cleavage than the sum total displayed at the Academy Awards **3.** functions that execs patronize to maintain their connections with other bigwigs or players who are loaded, and to make the "do-gooders who enjoy a nice tuna tartare hors d'oeuvres" scene; photos, which may appear in community society pages, are taken to document attendance. Such functions may often feature an awards portion, during which someone is honored, which really means that this person has been involved in the night's cause, but more important, that he could bring in the cash, i.e., people will buy tables out of a sense of obligation to the honoree when called by the honoree and asked to do so. **4.** formal function that facilitates furious **networking** and schmoozing, during which frisee salads with crumbled blue cheese and walnuts, lobster bisque, a chicken or fish entrée, and delicate chocolate bonbons with coffee will be served **5.** venue for the much-labored-over program for the evening, a slickly produced book that documents in writing all of the people who gave tremendous amounts of money to the sponsored organization. On occasion, should a table be paid for but lack attendants, favored employees (or in a pinch, the peons who worked until 1:00 A.M. proofing the program that nobody will read) will be offered the chance to attend, an offer they can't refuse, even though they are too tired, because it is viewed by management as a privilege or **"perk."** **6.** event where anyone who's not a bigwig is really there just for the **gift bag**

benefits 1. advantages to employment other than a base salary, such as health insurance, a 401k plan, etc. **2.** if you are a young employee, this is the last thing on your mind, and, in fact, you don't even understand what any of this means; you are young and don't think about disease and hardships like cancer and speeding cars that strike you down at random, or the possibility of dying penniless. **3.** if you are older, particularly if you have kids or a mortgage, this is all you think about, and this is the reason you keep your job despite the daily indignity and squashing of your dreams; if single, you contemplate working the system and marrying your dog to get him health benefits. **4.** the thing that enables you to keep working, given that it pays for your weekly shrink appointments and monthly psychopharmacologist visits, i.e., your **antidepressants 5.** what people who are freelancers by choice or by force are obsessed with, and rightly so, as no one seems to care if they become terminally ill or get hit by a car (or worse, have to spend six hundred dollars for a dentist appointment), and what those who have corporately subsidized health care don't think is an issue until they don't have benefits because they were downsized/rightsized/**fired**. *See also* **permalancer.**

best of breed 1. superior, the clear leader; used in reference to the delivery of products or services, or to an organization overall **2.** a meaningless title, as without exception it is used by a company to describe its *own* products and services; i.e., you will never hear the statement, "Well, Corpatron's software is best of breed, but we're a really close third." **3.** overused term in **sales** and **marketing** materials, **mission statements, KPI,** etc. *Also known as* best in class, world-class, first-class.

best personal regards 1. a closing, usually to an **e-mail** or letter, communicating good wishes **2.** "fuck you." *See also* **thanks, thanks in advance for your help.**

best practices 1. model approaches, systems, and processes that have been proven to be the most effective and are recognized industrywide **2.** a magic bullet of sorts (got a problem?: apply this and it will go away!), but also highly subjective. Not unlike **best of breed,** a company may say it implements best practices, but it can say whatever it wants to, and that doesn't necessarily make it true. But it sounds really good and gold-standardy.

big mother 1. condition that afflicts some employees who have been at a job for many years (more years than they can believe, than they can remember, etc.) and leads to a false sense of security, comfort, and the feeling that they are being well taken care of, due to seeing familiar characters and faces every day and enjoying reliable direct deposit, company parties, and affordable health care. They will unwittingly begin to see co-workers as **family,** view their company and its physical surroundings more like a college campus, and forget that their compensation is linked to performance—at which point they will be downsized (especially when the company realizes that the employee's job description hasn't changed in fifteen years, yet he receives an incredibly bloated salary, at which point Suzy from Joe Blow University will be hired to do the same job, but with more enthusiasm for a third of the pay).

big picture 1. overall view of an issue or matter **2.** lofty rationalization that **managers** use to justify their inflated salaries and the need for their **direct reports** to do all of the actual work on a project; also conveniently relieves them of the responsibility of having to think about details. *See also* **thirty-thousand-foot view.**

big tent 1. metaphorical space that can accommodate and is open and accepting of people of all types, interests, and beliefs **2.** a favorite of execs positioning their product, which may be traditionally (and probably actually) niche-oriented **3.** calls to mind both the circus and revivalist meetings, neither of which have much resonance in corporate culture, and besides, if the tent they were talking about really existed, it wouldn't take long before the northwest and southeast factions of the tent would be gearing up for a civil war

birthday 1. anniversary of one's birth **2.** at best, this will result in the tedious ritual of a greeting card being surreptitiously passed around the office for everyone to sign, regardless of their affection for or even knowledge of the recipient, leading to such yearbook-esque/empty sentiments as "Have a great one!" and "Best wishes!"; should the card get lost in its travels, an interdepartmental **e-mail** asking "Has anyone seen Julie's card? . . ." will clutter your inbox. **3.** at worst, an **e-mail** will go out taking up a collection to purchase a birthday gift for the coworker you don't know, inspiring you to rummage through your wallet for the spare singles you know will brand you as a cheap-ass, or debate the professional repercussions of just giving no money at all. N.B. If you do not give money, you will be intentionally excluded from the surreptitious circulation of the card and will not be able to sign it. **4.** yet another way to discern your place on the departmental food chain is based on if you get a gift, a card, or if your birthday passes unnoticed because no one gives a shit [*Please note:* the same rules follow for retirement, bridal and baby showers, extended vacations, etc.]

BlackBerry 1. handheld electronic device that can receive and send **e-mails** remotely **2.** now most commonly referred to as a "CrackBerry" due to its highly addictive nature, a device of the devil, as it allows anyone to contact you anywhere, even when you are out of the country **3.** source of an entirely new set of electronic etiquette, which includes responding within twenty-four hours of receiving a mes-

sage, not using one while in meetings (people do it anyway), and understanding/tolerating abrupt and curt responses **4.** most people who are allotted a BlackBerry will at first be very excited at the idea of having one and will whip it out all the time, and shortly thereafter will curse the day they received it and wish they were a waitress or toll booth operator.

blame 1. to assign fault or responsibility **2.** cornerstone of corporate culture; those who convincingly blame others for their own mistakes will advance quickly in an organization **3. managers** who are passionate advocates of accountability and taking responsibility will, ironically, often use this platform to invariably blame their employees for anything that goes wrong, i.e., it is never their fault no matter what. **4.** a behavior that weak, cowardly, and **unprofessional** people engage in on a daily basis, often resulting in the amusing spectacle of highly paid executives in business suits sitting around behaving like eight-year-olds. *See also* **passing the buck.**

blog 1. *abbr* Weblog; a Web site, often maintained by a single individual, consisting primarily of text and links to other sites, that is frequently updated **2.** provides a whole new and seemingly limitless batch of content to read while surfing the **Internet** at work; source of juicy **gossip,** entertainingly uncensored bitterness, and diversions to fend off **boredom** during the workday. Highly addictive, as checking one's favored blogs for updates can become a compulsion that will devour hours of your time **3.** pet project/the only forum you have to express yourself that you update at work; useful for venting frustration throughout the day

bonus 1. a sum of money received following the fourth quarter of the fiscal year to reward employees' performance **2.** what all of the completely miserable and disgruntled employees are enduring infinite misery and demoralization for at the end of the calendar year—if they've lasted this long, they're sure as hell going to get their check, goddammit; source of dead job market in December/January and flood of openings come spring **3.** particular source of angst for people in the financial industry, who with their bonus receive cutting **feedback** regarding their value to the company, which most likely does not reflect the eighteen-hour days they have worked, the damage to their relationships with their family and friends, related health problems, and the complete pricks whom they good-naturedly tolerate, and enable, on a daily basis **4.** delivering a bonus far less than what an employee expects is a classic **passive-aggressive** way to get rid of someone without the messiness of actually firing them, as they'll be so pissed they'll leave on their own, while saving the company a few bucks.

booth 1. a temporary physical structure created for the display of products or services **2.** cornerstone of the **trade convention;** a several-thousand-dollar structure that is essentially a shanty with corporate and product **logos** slapped all over it; ground zero for **premium** and business **card** distribution **3.** the place in which you will have to uncomfortably stand and talk to assorted industry folk for eight long, boring hours should you be charged with the responsibility of manning it; should your booth feature the appearance of **talent** in an attempt to create buzz or interest in one of your products, be prepared to suddenly act as crowd control or a bouncer and handle all the freaks who turn out to get an autograph or see a waning celebrity in the flesh. **4.** topic of intense debate and competition among **sales** and **marketing** people, who not only have strong opinions about how the booth should look and be laid out, but also keep the pissing contest of who has the best booth at the convention **top of mind**

boredom 1. a state of ennui caused by lack of stimulation **2.** crippling, mind-numbing condition extremely common in corporate America, in many cases because someone has *nothing to do,* whether because they are employed for forty hours a week to hang out until the two-hour **mission critical** task they were hired to do rolls around, or, more commonly, because their **boss** is a total control freak and **micromanager** who will not let them do the job they were hired to do or **delegate** any responsibilities. Should these employees receive an assignment, it will invariably be **busywork** or something that takes fifteen minutes to do, after which boredom will again take hold **3.** those who suffer boredom may be the most informed

people you know, based on countless hours spent reading every periodical on the Web; they become crackerjack literati, Snood, or solitaire players, and deeply resent every instance they are reprimanded for not being **on time,** because even though they have nothing to do, somehow it's really important that they not be late showing up to not do it.

boss 1. a supervisor **2.** a person, who through chance, a cruel twist of fate, etc., has authority over you and the ability to control you, tell you what to do, and make you feel like shit, simply because they hired you (i.e., not because they are smarter or can do a better job than you—in fact, they may have hired you so you can do their job for them). **3.** a person who, during the **interview** process and your first few days on the job, you convince yourself into thinking is "pretty cool," an idea you get over pretty fast

bottom line 1. the space on a financial statement that shows a venture's ultimate profit or loss **2.** the end result of anything, the upshot, the final analysis, the basic and important gist—a reference to that line on the financial statement; it should be noted that you or your department could be downsized to help make the numeric figure on the bottom line positive, not negative. *See also* **at the end of the day, net-net.**

brain dump 1. to communicate a large amount of information, particularly when handing off a project to someone else **2.** to have someone place a foot-high stack of files filled with their illegible and incomprehensible notes on your desk, clog your **e-mail** inbox with a dozen or so messages, and talk to you for twenty minutes about useless information regarding a project they've been working on for six months **3.** an act that will be followed by the statement, "So, is that clear? Do you have any questions?"—which is your only opportunity to get the information you will need regarding the project; of course, you don't have enough information to know what you will desperately need to know in two weeks, and the person who asks you this knows it and is, in fact, relying on it.

brain fart 1. the cause of an inexplicable and largely avoidable error, particularly regarding a simple matter **2.** despite its misleading name, a brain fart does not usually precede a **brain dump. 3.** a Get Out of Jail Free card; an excuse that relies heavily on the human condition and compassion of others, i.e., we are all fallible, and mistakes sometimes just happen, followed by an open and therefore hopefully endearing admission of **incompetence;** use of vulgarity adds a vaguely irreverent and lighthearted element to the explanation, ideally distracting from the stupid mistake in question. **4.** upon any reflection, not an acceptable excuse at all, as it provides no explanation whatsoever; may be caused by smoking too much pot or by heavy boozing the night before work. *Also known as* "I spaced" and "dropped the ball."

brainstorm 1. to generate ideas as a group in an accepting and open environment and in a free-form manner **2.** in an allegedly creative and nonjudgmental atmosphere, a supposedly relaxed forum in which **no idea is a bad idea**—that is, of course, until you generate a bad idea and are met with uncomfortable silence/looks that you are retarded or really uncool/the feeling that you are about to be fired **3.** a process that may pathetically involve "aids" to foster creativity such as exercises; dry-erase board/easel presence mandatory **4.** during these sessions, shrewd employees will typically withhold ideas, armed with the knowledge that they may add to their workload by sharing them.

brand 1. distinctive identity established through a **logo,** slogan, and/or the overall positioning of a product or company in a market **2.** major component of **perception:** if your brand is strong, but your product sucks, you're still ahead of the game; likewise, if your brand is trusted, you can probably get away with creating an inferior product by cutting a few corners to increase your **ROI. 3.** a subject of intense anthropomorphization: people will refer to the "soul" of the brand, the "spirit" of the brand, the "emotive aspects of the brand," etc., as well as the brand's "look and feel" (i.e., it's "irreverent," "playful," "reliable," etc.). *See also* **logo, brand refresh, rebrand.**

brand refresh 1. process of updating a company's identity, often through the modification of its **logo** or slogan **2.** a process that costs millions of dollars, requires thousands of hours of research assessing the psychological effects of variables such as shades of green/fonts, etc., and takes a ridiculously long time to complete **3.** a process that results in the decision to increase a **logo's** font size one point or move the company name to the other side of the logo graphic, which, amazingly, is what the newly hired exec who ordered the brand refresh wanted to do all along; will result in the waste of thousands of business **cards** and anything else on which the logo appears, due to an imperceptible change in the logo **4.** a very expensive and time-consuming process that may be immediately followed by a **merger** or acquisition, either of which will render all of the money and effort spent a complete waste

brick-and-mortar 1. a building; often used to describe the physical space that houses a retail operation **2.** a term born of the high-flying nineties Internet craze, which implied an almost primitive quality to the places where people bought things when they weren't spending untold zillions of dollars online, i.e., stores **3.** an environment that in the end proved shopping to be a lot more fun compared to buying things online due to the fact that customers can actually see and touch merchandise, avoid costly shipping and handling charges, and, most important, see and touch fellow patrons

bring to the table 1. to contribute or offer to a collaborative process or venture **2.** essentially, what a person or organization has—in the form of skills, knowledge, a relentless and desperately needed stranglehold on a market, a friendship dating back to high school with a key powerful exec, etc.—that affords them a place in the "dining room"; counterintuitively, not really related to what people have on their **plate 3.** when used to describe a single individual's contribution—either by the person themselves or someone else—this phrase imbues a sense of quality and importance far more than simply stating "I'm really good at X," "She cranks out **PowerPoint** presentations like no one I've ever seen," or "He really knows how to get **clients** loaded and make them forget the last time we totally blew it."

broadcast voicemail 1. a voicemail sent to all members of an organization via the assistance of the in-house telecommunications department **2.** first and foremost, due to the fact that broadcast voicemails are often delivered after normal working hours, or **COB**, it is a source of deep panic for all employees who come in in the morning and see a message waiting for them **3.** despite the occasional use of **talent** to deliver them in an attempt to make them more appealing, they are instantly deleted—usually before they even end—by relieved staffers still in the throes of a panic-induced adrenaline rush because they didn't triple-proofread the **memo** they sent out the night before.

Bschool 1. *slang:* business school; an academic institution one attends to receive a Master's Degree in Business, or MBA **2.** ground zero for the hatching and learning of vast amounts of corporate bullshit, which is then used to identify fellow Bschool attendees and make those who aren't feel stupid or just confused **3.** a place that ostensibly exists to increase a person's skills and knowledge of the business world and the theories surrounding it, but is really just a very expensive cocktail party where people go to make connections and buy the right to say **"At Stanford/Wharton/Princeton/Harvard . . ."**

budget 1. a monetary sum allotted to a project, department, etc. **2.** most of the time, if it's reserved for something that actually needs to get done, or to run the basic functioning of a department, this is a laughably low number; nevertheless, the expectation of the project, department, etc., will be nothing short of **excellence.** Meager budgets and extremely tight deadlines often go hand in hand. **3.** should an employee ask for a raise, the almighty "budget" will often be invoked in a scenario featuring **managers** grimly and contritely relating that the additional funds needed to increase a person's compensation are simply not "in it"; however, the five thousand dollars said employee is requesting is "in" the budget if it's needed to finance his four-night stay at the Four Seasons Tokyo (including minibar and blowfish sushi expenses) and round-trip **business class** airfare for the manager.

budget presentation 1. a formal and documented explanation of a business unit's financial needs for the coming fiscal year **2.** gen-esis of **managers** and department heads acting like desperate crazy people, as they must justify their existence and pathetically unjustifiable empire (read: extraordinarily bloated head count and operating **budget**); directly related to junior staffers working very late hours to compile, document, and artfully phrase (i.e., distort) data to support operating costs **3.** persuasive **budget** presentations will result in the approval of the addition of another staff position as well as more money for **T&E**, which is really the goal.

burn a bridge, to 1. the act of eliminating the positive affiliation between an employee and an employer; an act that jeopardizes the employee's chances of getting a positive reference when applying for a job elsewhere **2.** the reason many people do not flip out on their **bosses,** and try to make a clean exit no matter how much they hate their supervisor, citing "an opportunity I couldn't pass up" for their departure, which really means, "I hate your guts."

burnout 1. a state of emotional and physical exhaustion caused by a period of prolonged stress and frustration **2.** an inevitable corporate condition that can be caused by a very intense and trying short period of time (nine months working in a hellhole) or a long, drawn-out tenure at a job. Characterized by frequent displays of **unprofessional** behavior, a blithe refusal to do any work, and most important, a distinct aura of not giving a shit **3.** source of much amusement, as employees suffering from burnout are totally hilarious to watch and say all the things their coworkers are thinking

business class 1. premium airfare accommodations on airlines afforded to customers who pay premium prices, frequently used by executives **2.** what you will not be flying if you are not deemed special or "valuable" in the corporate hierarchy; wide seats, good food, nice treatment, free drinks and magazines, legroom, etc.; instead you will be relegated to a coach class middle seat sandwiched between two sweaty, gassy windbags who spend the flight hitting on you or interrupting your sleep as you suck down four packages of peanuts and a Diet Coke while watching *Miss Congeniality 2.*

business trip 1. travel mandated by the need to attend to company-related matters in a location other than where you work, financed by the employer's funds. **2.** *really, really* cool the first two times; you feel like someone important in the movies! You're taking a plane for free! You're eating out and saving the receipt for your **T&E!** You might even stay in a hotel that was written up in a magazine! **3.** anything after those two times: a pain in the ass requiring you to work weekends you aren't paid for/don't receive overtime or comp time for; forces you to leave the comfort of your life, home, and family and shove three days of belongings into a rolling travel bag; enter into the world of the dreaded **T&E,** which documents your every move; spend evenings wining and dining **clients** at **dinner 4.** an opportunity to glimpse how "the other .01 percent," i.e., senior management, lives, especially if you are traveling with them **5.** source of many man-hours of **administrative assistants** expensing the purchase of copies of *Marie Claire* and *Elle,* toothbrushes, and $3.00 bottled water for their boss, who is too lazy/thinks she is too important to fill out her own **T&E,** but who in reality would have a nervous breakdown if she was faced with the task of decoding and organizing all of her purchases and dealing with **accounts payable**

busted 1. *slang:* to be caught **2.** to be caught doing something that one should not be doing, and which one knows one should not be doing **3.** an event that is inevitable and for which there is no real recourse—if there was, the incident would not qualify as a true bust. Examples include: taking a **sick day** and being spotted having a beer at noon by your **boss;** enjoying a leisurely Sunday brunch with your top secret **office romance** and seeing one of your **direct reports;** claiming to your **manager** that you have spoken to a coworker about something you totally forgot about, and your manager getting to the person before you can, at which point it becomes clear you have lied

busywork 1. time-consuming tasks given to junior staffers **2.** the most boring, low-priority, frequently useless assignments given to junior employees, most often for the sole purpose of keeping them occupied and making the **manager** look good/justifying his bloated staff

because his "people" are doing things when in reality there is not enough real work to go around; will always be presented as an important task and may take the form of a job that has no conceivable ending, providing the **manager** with an ever-ready suggestion of what needs to be completed (e.g., "Have you finished project X yet?"). Examples include: filing invoices from the past ten years, data entry, creating a scrapbook of departmental projects, scanning every contract on file. *See also* **personal project.**

buttoned up 1. finalized; exceptionally professional in presentation **2.** a document, report, functioning of a department, etc., that appears virtually invulnerable to criticism or error and provides a formidable smoke-screen for the true chaos of the workplace **3.** a phrase that is particularly irritating because of its invocation of a puritanical and restrictive dress code, some chick dressed like Little Lulu, or the ubiquitous shirt-and-tie uniform foisted on men of the working world

buy-in 1. support, approval **2.** endorsement that if not secured, the doom of any project or idea is certain **3.** much schmoozing, angling, meeting, man-hours, and **PowerPoint presentations** are devoted to acquiring this blessing from senior **management;** the higher up on the food chain a buy-in is, the swifter something will get done, and those who have achieved it will remind you they have it with even greater frequency.

C

cafeteria **1.** company-housed place for buying breakfast and lunch that provides food service; possibly subsidized by corporation **2.** place to buy breakfast and lunch; possibly subsidized by corporation with the **goal** of making sure you never leave the building and, in the name of **efficiency**, eat out of a cardboard box in your **cube 3.** a place, among a desiccated salad bar, recycled chicken, and "creative" soups made from the leftovers of the past two days' entrees, that gives you a really good chance to check out your coworkers—how they look, who is hot, who they sit with, etc. Danger zone for seeing people you: have nothing to say to/can't explain the hell of the past six months of your job to on the sandwich line/haven't called back or are **avoiding 4.** site of extremely tempting instant gratification items such as jumbo chocolate chip cookies, which will make you feel, and quite possibly be, fatter and therefore not confident that you could ever get another job because you're repulsive **5.** home to some of the highest-quality people you see on a daily basis, the cafeteria workers, who actually know who you are, know your order, and refreshingly, do their job. Still, some may ask you four times if you want cheese on your turkey burger and give it to you sans cheese anyway.

call at 9:30 a.m./5:30 p.m. **1.** telephone call received at 9:30 in the morning or 5:30 in the evening **2.** total power play; common tactic of **micromanagers** and other assorted control freaks/petty **managers** who seem to be less concerned or occupied with doing their big important jobs than **busting** you for not being in the office—duties more suited to a babysitter or a third-grade teacher, both of which are paid *a lot less* than these people **3.** you will inevitably receive a call at the end of the day as you are shutting down your computer, even though you have done virtually nothing all day and have been waiting for a reply from your **boss** on a matter you addressed many hours/days ago—NOW they're ready; the issue they contact you about will often be of the lowest priority or even a faux issue, i.e., they are just calling to see if you are there, and, in fact, the *only* reason you are there is to answer the phone when they call. *Also see* **facetime.**

call out 1. an observation **2.** **feedback** dressed-up in a **passive-aggressive** form; what you hear when you did something wrong, or how someone tells you they would do a job differently, whether their idea is better or not

caller ID 1. the digital display on a phone that identifies the number from which a call originates **2.** so cool; provides the all-important function of identifying the **boss's** call, the annoying friend's call, the potential employer's call, and offers the added bonus of acting as a pop quiz on area codes nationwide

3. adds another level of call screening, so that by the time an **administrative assistant** picks up the phone, they have already identified you as someone the exec they work for doesn't want to talk to

candy 1. small confections **2.** the crack of the workplace **3.** an empty-calorie food item that in the economy of the workplace skyrockets in value, far outweighing its worth in the outside world **4.** common booty of the **3:45 run**

candy dish 1. a container that holds confections **2.** a powerful magnet that draws employees from all locations on a department or floor; locus for threadbare ritual of people noticing the contents ("Oh, someone brought candy"), feigning hesitation regarding taking a piece ("I really shouldn't. I'm such a cow already."), and finally "giving in" ("Looks like more time on the treadmill for me tonight!")— even though they are not going to the gym after work anyway. These people will be back later to further deplete the contents of the dish **3.** excellent tool for meeting people and making them feel indebted to you if it's located in your **cube** or **office,**

as word will get around quickly where the **candy** is coming from and *everyone* will stop by to get some, but will be forced into talking to you, the keeper of the candy, in an attempt to make it seem they actually like you, not just the candy; also useful in that it becomes clear who lacks self-control or is greedy. Costs of constantly refilling the candy dish can be defrayed by hitting post-holiday sales at the local drugstore, where seasonal **candy** is sold at 50 percent off. **4.** place to observe **candy** addicts, who will arrive at the dish for the fifth time that day, only to be met with the bottom of the barrel, i.e., what is left after anything that even remotely contains chocolate is gone (old-school root beer, butterscotch, or strawberry hard candy that nobody wants), but will take something anyway

card, my 1. business card **2.** major source of deforestation, as simply spitting on someone will result in them handing you their card, particularly at **networking** events; especially annoying people will distribute their card in the line at the grocery store or at funerals **3.** status symbol that is subject of bizarre corporate pornography fixated on variations in card stock, font, printing (raised or no?), etc. **4.** really exciting rite of passage for junior employees when they reach a level so they can order them; some overanxious tykes may order those cards online or at Kinko's, but those don't really look the same, now do they? **5.** awesome and convenient way to enter raffles for a free **lunch** at a restaurant or at **trade conventions 6.** errors in the spelling of one's name, **title,** extension, etc., will result in the need to reorder and a six-month delay in getting replacements; similarly, events such as **mergers,** moving, or the redesigning of a **logo** will necessitate the destruction of several thousand business cards per employee and an interminable wait for replacements **7.** forum for some of the most inspired work ever executed by employees, who get "creative" with their job **titles** while still managing not to lie, exactly, e.g., Junior Technical Operative equals photocopy repair guy, Enterprise Solutions **Manager** means anything a person wants it to mean.

carpool 1. an arrangement through which participants collectively share the work and burden of a **commute** as a group, including driving and paying for related costs such as gas and tolls **2.** a necessary evil geared toward cutting the cost of getting to and from work, that no participant really wants to be a part of, i.e., if they could afford to get to work in their own bubble of privacy and cone of silence, you bet your boots they would. **3.** a really great way to draw out the workday even more, by surrounding yourself with coworkers/people from your office, that is not only subject to potential **office politics,** but petty and endlessly annoying carpool politics as well as a whole host of problems like the person who is always late, the person who always smells, the person who insists on eating a McGriddle/drinking **coffee** and getting it all over the car, the person who always shorts everybody on cash, and, perhaps the worst: the person who never shuts up

casual Friday 1. a policy that allows employees to adopt less formal dress on the last day of the workweek **2.** what is viewed by the company as a **perk,** but really makes you wish that everyone was required to wear a suit all the time; results in the true "fashion sense" of staffers being expressed in an ocean of pleated khakis paired with tucked-in "sea foam green" Polo, cutoff jeans shorts (and their extremely revealing cousin, "Daisy Dukes"), flip-flops, denim shirts sporting embroidered company **logos,** visible belly rings and chains, half shirts, and anything terry cloth or spandex. **3.** will inevitably result in a companywide **memo** defining the parameters of "casual," which essentially says, "We didn't think we were at a roadside truck stop on the interstate, but come on, people. Show some class." Will include the phrase "a reminder of what is appropriate . . ."

cc 1. *lit* carbon copy **2.** an option available in **e-mail** programs that allows people to "copy" other recipients' names and display these names to the primary addressee/s **3.** a technique used to make a message officially on the record and basically put more power behind the **e-mail** than it would have if you sent it on your own; a classic **CYA** move **4.** a **passive-aggressive** indicator that things have gotten slightly hostile between the writer and the recipient (i.e., previous messages have been sent without the cc, but at some point they appear, because a message is going unanswered/being **avoided,** or the exchange has become vaguely abusive) **5.** an instrument of control freaks and **micromanagers** who insist they be cc'd on *every **e-mail** you send,* so they know what you are doing at all times and can reprimand you for making the smallest errors in your missives

celebrate 1. to uphold and recognize with great pride **2.** something execs and companies are very fond of doing regarding intangibles such as **diversity** and an organization's **culture,** especially because it doesn't really cost anything to do so **3.** if celebrating does cost money, it will be the employee's money that is spent on an **outing** not subsidized by the company, e.g., "Please join me in celebrating our success with a gathering at TGIFriday's this Tuesday. I hope to see you all there."

CEO 1. *acronym* Chief Executive Officer **2.** the top banana, who gets paid more money in one year than you will ever, ever see in your lifetime. May very well have no idea what is going on in the company; may very well have his own private jet **3.** sometimes attractive, affable figurehead who's good for making

appearances on *Charlie Rose* and CNN to chat about the company's **vision** and its **culture**

CFO 1. *acronym* Chief Financial Officer **2.** the dude (see **glass ceiling**) who holds the purse strings at the top of the **org chart;** prime minister to the **CEO's** role as monarch **3.** may very well have every idea of what is going on in the company; may very well be doing everything he can to hide it, in the form of cooking the books (while riding in his own private jet)

challenge 1. formidable obstacle **2.** a serious problem no one has the answer to yet

challenging 1. difficult **2.** hard, or, in some cases, impossible. In a worst-case scenario (e.g., no one is buying your company's product and the business is tanking) this will still be the strongest word ever used to describe the situation. **3.** a good code word to whip out when complaining to your **boss** about someone so you don't seem like a whiner/big baby, but still want them to know that you're about to clock a coworker, e.g., "I'm finding working with Sharon quite challenging"; also good for describing your "weaknesses" (read: things you have no idea how to do/stink at) in a job **interview**

champion 1. to personally support with great commitment **2.** employed by people in **leadership** positions, or those who would really like to play one on TV; often used in the context of **meetings,** with several attendees on hand to serve witness to one's **passion 3.** to espouse with fervent advocacy and forget about immediately after leaving the room; may be followed up by an **e-mail** or **meeting** to further reinforce the backer's pledge, after which you will never hear about the issue again

change 1. the result when something undergoes alteration or passes from one state to another **2.** look out, dude—it's never good: heads will roll, new annoying policies will be instituted, **consultants** will lurk behind conference room doors, etc. **3. managers** will be strong **advocates** of embracing change, which is just them telling their employees that change is going to happen whether they like it or not, so they might as well act really psyched about it, otherwise they'll be identified as a pocket of resistance or someone with a bad attitude who's not a **team player. 4.** in **a merger** or partnership situation, euphemism for people getting downsized; the very same **managers** who advocated embracing change (because they thought they were untouchable) may very well find that they have embraced themselves right out of a job. **5.** foundation of the entire industry of **change management 6.** subject of the slim self-helpy business tome *Who Moved My Cheese?* which didactically employs a story about little mice to illustrate the appropriate way to relate to change, and the consequences that befall those mice who don't (which you may be forced to read). Note: the book is a runaway best-seller due to the fact that it's about twelve pages long, illustrated, and can be easily read in one sitting in **business class.**

change management 1. overseeing the process of change or transition in an organization **2. consultant** lingo for "cutting away the dead wood," i.e., laying you off. An ugly process that senior management **farms out** to consulting firms so that the execs don't have to deal with the messy business of restructuring

checking in 1. to contact someone regarding an issue previously discussed **2. passive-aggressive** intro to **e-mail** or phone call roughly translated as "I know you have not done this or are **avoiding it,** so I am hounding your ass about it". **3.** when qualified by "just" (i.e., "just checking in"), becomes more timid; often used by an employee in a lesser position than the recipient. Roughly translated as "I know you don't have time for this/don't want to do it/or forgot about it, but my **boss keeps** asking me about it, and if you could just throw me a bone telling me that it's **moving forward,** it would buy me a little time. Do you think we might have an answer in a month . . . or so? It is the highest honor to have the opportunity to be neglected by you. **Best personal regards**".

circle back 1. revisit an issue or question. **2.** A way of saying, "I don't have time to deal with this right now, so I'll put you at number thirty-six on my 'to do' list, and when you rise to the top, if ever, I'll be in touch." Also: "I'm not sure if this is worthy of my concern. Let me talk to eight people who are impossible to get an answer out of, and when I hear from them, I'll be in touch. Like in four years maybe."

circular file 1. the garbage can **2.** the garbage can

cleaning lady 1. a female member of the custodial staff **2.** a person, who for "some reason" always seems to be a woman, who surfaces after **COB** to empty the trash cans in every office, vacuum, and nonjudgmentally pick up the massive amount of garbage employees generate in a single day; often a person of color or an immigrant who you can just tell curses the corporate masses she cleans up after, but *really needs the job,* and so adopts a deferential manner/ tries to be **invisible 3.** employees who frequently work late may come to feel they know her very well through the continual exchange of "Hi. Thank you. Have a good night," or at least find her reliable presence comforting; will be slightly traumatized if a new cleaning lady suddenly appears. If the cleaning lady and an employee also speak the same language other than English, they may conduct conversations about how bad their jobs are in it. **4.** some white-collar workers will feel really great about themselves for engaging in small talk with "a little person" even though they have nothing to gain from her; others will act as if the cleaning lady is not there because they have nothing to gain from her, and they really just want to be left alone while they surf the Web after hours.

client 1. a party that has hired another to produce goods or services **2.** given that they are paying the bills, they are afforded almost mythic status and in mixed company are spoken of with tones of awe, fear, and reverence (e.g., "I need this for *the client*" or "*The client* has requested we avoid that topic"). **3.** in a creative environment, when presented with ideas in a pitch **meeting,** will inevitably favor the safest/least-inspired concepts, or worse, will have a **brainstorm** that combines several wildly incompatible approaches, or will get really excited about a completely new idea of their own that sucks (further proving that the customer is *not* always right) **4.** behind closed doors, the cause of much eye-rolling, ridicule, exasperation, and liberal use of choice profanities **5.** demand **excellence** and copious amounts of

work but are not willing to pay for it, and revel in their economically dictated position of power **6.** recipient of many **gift baskets**

clique 1. a small exclusive social group **2.** you went to high school, you know how it is: really annoying clusters of people who are bonded to each other as much by the fact that they are keeping people out as the idea that they may possibly like each other—but at work, it's that much more pathetic because all of those involved are adults. **3.** very common among entry-level staffers, as they don't really have that much important going on at work (e.g., something other than caring that the temp has weird hair), they may still somewhat resemble what they looked like in college, they're going out drinking together/trying to get laid, and are not big enough players to engage in **office politics,** the adult equivalent/400-level seminar of cliques.

closed-door meeting 1. a gathering of a sensitive nature held in the confines of an **office** during which the door is shut **2.** the shit is hitting the fan; someone is getting an ass-whipping, getting **fired,** being confronted about illegal, abusive behavior that has gone unnoticed forever and is now having dire consequences that have trickled up to management, or perhaps, he is just getting a **performance review; HR** is frequently on the scene. **3.** senior management is sitting around for five hours with a catered **lunch** reviewing **budgets** and talking about who is expendable in preparation for downsizing **4.** people having sex

closure 1. a sense of finality or ending **2.** this is something people often say they want to "achieve" or "get some" of, which really means, "You know, I just want this to be over and done with so we can forget about it and act like it never happened"; usually implies some kind of mutual understanding through which all parties are satisfied, but it more likely indicates that the senior staff member wanting to get it has decided that the issue at hand is never going to be talked about again.

coach 1. a professional hired to facilitate the growth of a **manager** through observing his performance, soliciting **feedback** from coworkers, and recommending areas for development **2.** coaching is a totally BS job that

is a money geyser for the professionals hired to do it that usually produces no results. Often reserved for the worst managers in an attempt to rehabilitate them/keep the company from getting sued; sort of an exclusive **EAP** for managers—but a lot more expensive

COB/EOB 1. *acronyms* close of business and end of business, respectively; the end of the workday **2.** employed as a deadline for materials or information needed, which is meant to indicate delivery around the 5:00 P.M. hour, but widely open to creative interpretation by procrastinators everywhere, e.g., by the literal end of the day, 12:00 midnight; by 9:00 A.M. the next day; or when the day in question is a Friday, it really means by 9:00 A.M. Monday

coffee 1. a naturally caffeinated beverage created through the process of infusing ground coffee beans with hot water **2.** the key word here being *caffeine* **3.** a bitter, kind of nasty-tasting, often tepid and disgusting beverage that millions of people have convinced themselves is a warm and tasty elixir of love **4.** fuel that not surprisingly is often offered free of charge at many workplaces, albeit in an amazingly putrid form—but hey, it's free. Gratis coffee can all too easily lead an otherwise manageable one- or two-cup-a-day habit spiraling out of control into a five- or six-cup-a-day habit, which can result in a lot of people walking around the office like they're on crack. **5.** lack of coffee will often serve as a scapegoat for people saying really stupid things prior to 10:00 A.M. ("Sorry! Haven't had my coffee yet!")

cold shoulder 1. intentional disregard **2.** your previously friendly and affable **boss** or **colleague** suddenly starts ignoring you, leaving you with the sense that you are being punished for something that you may or may not be aware of; may inspire the feeling you are **"in trouble"**; very eighth grade. **3.** a behavior frequently employed by a **boss** who has recently received **notice** that an employee is leaving because, of course, only the **boss** is allowed to be ambitious and desire a career, and the need to move on is a personal affront to them, selfish, and flat-out just not acceptable; plus they're such a great **boss,** and why would you ever want to leave your post of serving them and their needs and being their

battery cell? **4.** a noncommunicative way of setting boundaries after an **office romance** gone sour, a late night of drinking that resulted in inappropriate conversation, and/or one that abandoned the dictates of corporate social hierarchy, a job well done that made someone look bad, etc.

colleague 1. a coworker **2.** a fancy way of saying "someone I work with"; usually implies that the person referred to is on the same rung of the food chain as the person employing the term, i.e., they're not the boss or an **assistant.** "My colleague" is really something only doctors or professors should whip out—unlike, say, merchandising staffers.

coming along 1. making progress or developing positively **2.** a casual assessment of the status of a project, which really means "I haven't started it yet, but after this conversation I'm going back to my desk to find that file/**e-mail** and try to remember what you wanted so I don't **bust** myself by having to ask you about a project I'm claiming to have almost done."

committee 1. a group created to address a specific topic or issue

2. very annoying, inefficient forum created to attend to a specific matter of business, typified by petty power plays among members and **meetings** that seem to take place every other day, in which nothing is ever decided; common product of **initiatives,** in which case voluntary participation is a primo way to **kiss ass 3.** an excellent tool for maintaining job security, as their existence can span many months, i.e., if you get on the **brand refresh** or **merger**-integration committee, you're guaranteed at least nine more months of a steady paycheck. *See also* **subcommittee.**

commute 1. to make the journey to and from work; may also be the journey itself, i.e., a person's "commute" **2.** may be the best part of your workday, because you are not dealing with your coworkers; may also be an extremely excruciating experience because you must sit in your car for an hour in traffic, stand next to a foul-smelling person on the bus or train, **carpool** with people who you can't stand who you are bound to by the cruel twist of fate that you work at the same place and live near each other **3.** may be the most intellectually stimulating part of your day if you listen to NPR, or the reason someone is filing a **sexual harassment** suit against you if you listen to Howard Stern **4.** source of unspoken politics regarding seat ownership and awkward familiarity with the people you see *every day* on the 5:20 bus, train, etc., who you don't really know, but feel like you know; upon seeing these people in "real life," you will be struck with the sense that you are seeing a good friend, but then realize it's just that guy from the second-row window seat. **5.** employees who travel from the suburbs will use their commute as an excuse to not come in, **work from home,** or leave early at the slightest indication of inclement weather; they act all serious and concerned about it, but everyone knows they're blowing off work

company car 1. one vehicle, in a fleet employed under contract by an organization, to be used for official company business **2.** totally sweet; black Lincoln Town Cars with clean interiors that will ferry you home or to the airport, and you don't even have to tip the driver—a for-real **perk.** Downsides include the fact that they are always late, must often be shared with coworkers, and don't include minibars.

compelling 1. to demand one's attention; captivating **2.** a word that has no place in the corporate world and is indicative of senior management's condescending delusion that they can devise/orchestrate an idea that speaks to a company on a meaningful level and ultimately affects behavior; may be used in conjunction with **vision** or **goals**

concern 1. interested or troubled **2.** if someone is concerned about something you have done, this is their way of saying they are pissed about it; they do not really care about you or what you have to say on the matter; a common management trope, employed to soft-pedal an ass-whipping **3.** if someone is expressing concern for you, you are likely behaving in an extremely erratic manner, be it in the form of public breakdowns, going ballistic on a **colleague,** or never showing up for work. If your **boss** says this to you, consider yourself extremely fortunate to have a supervisor who may actually care about your well-being, but also note that you are probably

highly skilled, as you would just be **fired** if you weren't in some way valuable to the company.

conference 1. large-scale gathering of professionals convened for the purpose of exchanging information through activities such as panels, lectures by gurus and guest speakers, and seminars dedicated to industry-related topics **2.** an industry-themed gathering of professionals with a title like, "So What's This Internet Thing All About, and How Can You Make Money Off of It?"; an excuse to not go to work that may involve taking a **business trip,** but is less demanding than attending a **trade convention**— which means you can look up your buddies from college and go out drinking without too much consequence. An event similar to a **trade convention** in that much free booze will be consumed and **office romances** and affairs will be born or continue

conference call 1. telephone call that involves multiple participants **2.** extremely boring, sometimes marathon-long events that, in any form, drive home the alienating behemoth of technology used in the name of efficiency; variants include the "call-in," which through the use of a phone number and an access code can be done from one's desk, and the group call, which involves many people gathered in a **conference** room, looking at and speaking into a pod that has a form reminiscent of a spaceship interpreted by Hasbro **3.** a call-in can actually be an event to look forward to, as it offers an opportunity to **multitask,** surf the **Internet,** and make gratuitous use of the mute button. Group calls are marked by much eye-rolling, drafting non–work related "to do" lists, doodling, and paying the least amount of attention possible to the conversation while still listening for the mention of your name; should you be caught unawares in this last scenario, a simple, "I'm sorry, could you repeat that?/I couldn't hear you/ You're breaking up on this end" will give you plenty of time to recover **4.** as a junior staffer you may be asked to sit in on a conference call, meaning you are not an active participant who can provide **feedback,** aside from the most basic information or scripted points from your **boss;** this is your **boss** saying, "This is going to be really boring and I don't want to do it, so you will"; the three hours of your workday spent on the call will be reduced to a four-sentence **e-mail** summarizing the proceedings, to the neglect of all the high-priority projects you are working on. Even though you have lost valuable time at the request of your **boss,** you will still be reprimanded for possessing inadequate **time management** skills. **5.** a call-in may be utilized to facilitate a **town hall,** which, of course, makes employees feel so much more connected to what's going on at the company; if you have a really cool **boss,** pizza and beer will be ordered for this event to make it go down easier. *Please note:* many an employee has been **busted** because they started bad-mouthing someone on the other end of the line before the person hung up, so just make sure they have.

confidential 1. of a secret and sensitive nature **2.** not applicable in a corporate environment; nothing is ever confidential, and the sooner this is understood, the better; sounds more official than **off the record,** but is equally unreliable **3. HR** people love to invoke this, e.g., "You know that everything we discuss here is confidential," which really means, "Anything you say from here on out is fair game for me to take directly to your **boss,**

or to show up on the company **Intranet.**"

constructive criticism 1. feedback that is not positive, but is presented in a healthy and useful manner with the ultimate aim of providing an employee with insight into how they can develop, and supporting them in their effort to do so **2.** a term that is applied by the person using it, making it therefore completely subjective and ultimately meaningless, e.g., your **boss** says, "This looks like shit" and considers this constructive criticism, so it is **3.** a phrase that is more about how it is received than how it is delivered, i.e., if you sit there and appear to be listening attentively or take notes while **zoning out,** and express total agreement and gratitude for the **feedback,** it is constructive criticism. Someone who claims to take constructive criticism well will also profess **I like people/I'm a people person.**

consultant 1. an outside party professing to have an area of expertise, brought in to offer a fresh perspective on an organization. Boasts a **résumé** listing multiple high-profile **clients;** is skilled at using jumbo Magic Markers and easel-mounted paper. Likes to talk about their bicoastal existence and the hotel rooms they are living in—which are nicer than your apartment—on the company dime. May present themselves as "down-home" and folksy or of the social worker ilk to engender your trust and honesty. However, it is important to remember that these people are ultimately not on your side, as you are not paying their salary. **2.** an outside party brought in to do the dirty work. If there are consultants lurking in your company—particularly those representing large firms—brush up your **résumé** because the ax is falling soon. Kind of like androids, consultants will come into a company to evaluate an organization's **process** and overall efficiency, and then tell senior management who they need to fire. Consultants may approach you to discuss your process with them, but they're actually determining if you are expendable. **3.** extremely highly paid individuals because they do two things that executives will go out of their way to avoid: delivering bad **feedback** to other senior execs, and firing people. Black belts in corporate bullshit; very big on **adding-value,**

specialize in **change management**

co-opt 1. to take and use as one's own; appropriate **2.** a tactic frequently used in **marketing** that usually involves big corporations researching and/or raiding a subculture and slapping the investigated group's language (often slang) or aesthetic on a product or campaign to make it seem cool or **edgy** to the group itself or less-hip mainstream consumers; downright embarrassing how often multi-million/billion-dollar companies that are run by a lot of suburban white guys rip off hip-hop and youth culture

copy machine 1. device used to reproduce documents **2.** miracle of technology at the core of everyday business; also fierce, testy, and temperamental beasts; enemy of **administrative assistants** and secretaries around the globe **3.** only malfunction when something extremely important is needed (as will their close cousins, the printers); those employees who can rehabilitate these machines in a time of crisis, through simply reading manuals, brute force, or replacing paper, are destined for management positions, as they are problem-solvers. **4.** source of the major **perk** of free copies (of **résumés** [remember to take the original off of the glass], party invitations, tax forms, etc.), as anyone unemployed will tell you, Kinko's ain't that cheap; color copier on-site is a major score and a legitimate argument for tolerating a horrible job.

core competency 1. the strengths of a person or organization **2.** what a person or organization is good at; much time will be spent trying to figure out a company's core competencies so its managers can forget about the things they suck at and try to make as much money on the things they can actually do well. **3.** it's worth pointing out that *anything* can be a core competency, and the people who talk about them know this, e.g., "On Friday, my core competency is sucking down beers with my coworkers at the bar around the corner from my office." **4.** like **skill set,** will be discussed heavily during a **performance review**

corporate art 1. fine art purchased by a company for display at its facilities **2.** often extremely ugly art that art history majors who once had fantasies of running their own galleries help procure for large companies while also respectfully explaining why a freakin' canvas with some paint on it is so expensive or that a work's ability to match peach-colored walls is perhaps not the best way to select a piece **3.** status symbols purchased for display in the corporate **HQ** lobby and on executive floors; floors or buildings occupied by worker bees with be decorated with **Successories,** or nothing at all

corporate communications 1. department responsible for the company's interface with the media as well as the dissemination of information within an organization **2.** generator of: all of the **mass e-mails** that you delete without reading; the **town hall;** the **CEO's** rosy appearance on CNN/*Charlie Rose,* and the write-ups that proclaim him as a "vanguard" in *Time* and *Business Week;* announcements regarding recent **layoffs** or **mergers;** any company speech you hear; the company newsletter/**Intranet** site; etc. **3.** ministers of information, PhDs in corporate bullshit; do not trust or believe anything these people say. **4.** at heart, **PR people** who are masters of spin and will dodge any bullet shot at them while making everything at the company seem great; really hard-core because they are indispensable to and are in the pocket of the **CEO** and provide the exec with crucial talking points

corporate roadkill 1. employees who have lost their jobs as a result of a **merger** or the creation of a partnership **2.** the poor suckers who did not dodge the bullet of rightsizing, smartsizing, downsizing, etc., as a direct result of a **merger** or the creation of a partnership; allusion to dead animals on the side of the highway is very appropriate, as employees who have worked for a company for fifteen years will be cut loose, and no one will look back to see if they're okay, because no one has the time or inclination to deal with a rancid corpse on the corporate highway and are just glad they weren't hit by the Mack truck of progress or efficiency.

cost center 1. a sector or department of an organization that is necessary for the operation of a company and does not generate revenue or directly impact profits **2.** the second-class citizens of the corporate world: **accounts**

payable, creative services, catering, etc., subject to overt elitism from employees who work in revenue-generating centers **3.** breeding ground for **micromanagers,** who greatly inflate the importance of their work in an unconscious reaction to the knowledge that, in reality, when compared to other areas of the business, their work isn't important at all

creative/noncreative divide 1. the different work styles of those in more artistically influenced departments and those in more analytical and business-related areas **2.** the "artists" think they are the **"talent"** in the equation, the lifeblood of the company, and use the excuse of their **process** to explain sloppy work habits and general prima donna behavior, even if they are, say, designing a direct mail piece for As Seen on TV products or writing copy for an in-house piece that no one outside the company will ever see; usually can work this angle so they are not as accountable as their noncreative colleagues, which of course engenders great animosity toward the creatives; the revenue centers, like **sales,** may in reality be the lifeblood of the company, and therefore while they may not receive the cod-

dling the creatives do, they relish knowing they have the last laugh because they make *a lot more money* than the creatives and know that if they screw up, the artists are out of a job. **3.** to the creatives, the business folk seem like uptight, rigid pawns who have sold their soul to The Man and are too plebeian to understand what they are saying; to the business sect, the creatives seem like lazy, sloppy, and flaky narcissists who remind them of the kids in the drama club at high school who smoked pot, wore weird clothes, were somewhat full of shit, and now are vaguely pathetic given that they, too, have sold out to The Man, but delude themselves into thinking they haven't—and they make less money while they're at it. Ha.

critical path 1. the sequence of actions essential to the achievement of an organization's **goals 2.** most useful for determining what you *don't* need to do rather than what you do; if it's not a critical path issue, you can blow it off for a long time, ideally for as long as it takes to get another job, when it ceases to be your problem.

crying 1. to shed tears **2.** first and foremost a sign of weakness, particularly for men (because you know, women are weak, so when they cry it's not exactly a surprise) **3.** although through injustice, frustration, **hate,** and humiliation (or the breakup of an **office romance**) you will be moved to do this in public at some point or another, it's really not a good idea, even if you are going through a divorce, the illness of a loved one, etc.—AKA sometimes normal life events. No one will remember the circumstances that made you cry, they'll just remember the crying, which is a sign that you are deeply flawed or mentally unstable or, um . . . (what is that word?) right!: human—a definite liability in the workplace. **4.** verboten activity that results in desperate and often futile attempts to recover, such as retreating to the **bathroom** to splash cold water on one's face, attending to teary eyes with sandpaper-like takeout napkins stashed in the back of a desk drawer, and, in the case of women, applying copious amounts of makeup in the form of mental breakdown camouflage. *See also* **employee assistance program, therapy, antidepressant.**

cube 1. a work area designed for one person, delineated by partitions on the left, right, and opposite sides, most often containing a small desk area, computer, and phone **2.** the institutionally hued small piece of real estate most often allotted to junior employees, that people who have **offices**—and therefore some amount of privacy and protection from roaming staffers—feel aren't really that bad **3.** that rare zone where attempts to express one's individuality may be permitted. This may take the form of tacking up: snapshots of significant others shown in a fleeting moment of happiness (due to rampant **homophobia** in the workplace, most often of the hetero variety), six sorority sisters who look exactly alike out at a bar, or a beautiful vista, which means "This is where I'd rather be"; Dilbert cartoons that depict a company's dysfunctionality precisely; printouts that proclaim "witty" sentiments such as "I hate Mondays," "Every dog has its day. Today is not your day," and "What part of 'No' don't you understand?" Cube inhabitants who are particularly frustrated by their station, both in the **office** and in life, will go overboard, announcing their creativity with elaborate displays of decorative wrapping paper, evidence of their "real **passion**" (Broadway musicals, Tom Cruise, their own artwork, posters for their band's gigs, etc.), an army of tchotchke-like action figures or snowglobes, a tropical fish tank, and the like. **4.** an area that, while designated to a single employee, is routinely regarded as public space in which to have loud and inane conversations, lean or hang on, and liberally borrow **office supplies** without the owner's consent

culture 1. the predominant attitudes and behavior of a group **2.** lots of lip service is given to the notion of a company's culture, as well as nurturing it, because it's supposedly so healthy and awesome. However, it's really just the specific and unique ways in which an organization is dysfunctional and screwed up, and a random product of all of the neuroses and insecurities of the people who work there. **3.** foundation for many of the nonsensical unspoken rules regarding behavior and communication particular to an organization, department, etc., that you will know you have violated when people act really uncomfortable after you say or do something that, in real life, is totally normal. These employees may try to explain why you have just violated a sacred corporate tenet, but in most cases will stop short of doing so, as they can't bring themselves to verbalize the lunacy they are advocating and know it makes them sound really stupid. *See also* **just so you know.**

customer-centric 1. to be focused on the needs of the people paying for goods or services **2.** something companies declare they are now, as if they didn't have to be in the past; a label that is applied with zero effort and needs zero **follow-up** if the **marketing** and **corporate communications** departments are any good **3.** not unlike **best of breed** in that no company is going to claim they are not customer-centric

customer is always right, the 1. service-oriented adage placing the requests and needs of the consumer above all else **2.** a patently false and venomous idea that anyone who has ever worked in a service capacity will adamantly refute; particularly common in the food service industry; the lower an employee is positioned on the totem pole, the more they will despise this concept. **3.** root of some of the most petty, obnoxious, greedy, and entitled behavior from people who claim to be members of the human race and act as though the employees assisting them are their personal servants and they themselves are a visiting dignitary because they're buying a T-shirt or the Thrilling Three breakfast special; those who live by this theory will often ask to "speak to a **manager**," as if they are summoning the president of the United States, and will not rest until they are given something for free. **4.** a truly irresponsible idea that encourages the most base instincts of humanity; whoever made it up should be shot. *See also* **client.**

Cute, thin, not-that-smart chick who laughs a lot and whom everybody loves (CTNTSCWL-WEL) 1. a woman you work with **2.** infuriating to any woman who does not aspire to be part of a *Maxim* photo spread or believes that her intelligence and hard work should speak for themselves as well as to men who are not **MQNWSMEWGAB-HANG 3.** adopts the pose that she is really serious about her work and would take horrified

offense at the suggestion that she is **leveraging** the dumb non-threatening broad archetype to her advantage; especially maddening because even respected married men holding managerial positions, known for their objective manner, get all cheesy and flirty when simply talking to this person **4.** gets away with anything, purveyor of office **gossip,** and will act like your new best friend if she thinks you have something to offer her, but also expert practitioner of the **cold shoulder;** needless to say, not to be trusted farther than you can throw her—an urge that is frequent and actually might be fun to try sometime

CV 1. *Latin* curriculum vitae, a **résumé**. *See* **résumé.**

CYA 1. *acronym* Cover Your Ass **2.** essential corporate survival tactic, as it enables one to deflect **blame** and avoid getting **busted;** can be achieved in a variety of ways, including **FYI e-mails,** the use of **cc** or **bcc,** and befriending the **receptionist**

D

················

deck 1. *slang:* a **PowerPoint** presentation **2.** a term derived from the fact that this is a collection of successive "slides" and therefore like a deck of cards **3.** a term that should be derived from the fact that "deck" can also mean "to hit or knock down," as in, "That deck was so boring it essentially rendered me unconscious."

deep bench strength 1. the involvement of highly qualified and experienced employees **2.** a very stupid way of saying highly qualified and experienced employees are involved in a project

deets 1. *slang:* details **2.** an extraordinarily annoying way of saying "details"; often used regarding information someone will provide, e.g., "Send me the deets," "**E-mail** me the deets," etc. *Also see* **co-opt.**

delegate 1. to assign the responsibility and execution of a task to someone else **2.** a case of feast or famine. Some **managers** delegate everything to their staff, which affords them the time to surf the **Internet,** take long **lunches,** and talk on the phone all day while their underlings do all the work they will ultimately take credit for. Other **managers,** charged with the job of overseeing the work of a department and thinking about the **big picture,** will be total control freaks and **micromanagers** who hoard all work that has any meaning or value whatsoever, leaving only **busywork** for their staff, a management style that is grossly inefficient and may result in people with master's degrees having filing projects as their primary responsibility.

delight the customer 1. to serve the recipient of a product or service beyond their expectations **2.** oh come on—*delight?* When was the last time in your life you were personally "delighted" by anything? 1985? Most likely, it had more to do with copping a feel than achieving a **KPI,** unless your **KPI** at the time involved intimately interfacing with the hot goth chick from AP English.

deliverable 1. something that is produced as a result of an agreement **2.** what will be produced according to the terms a contract, strategic plan, etc.; **goals** that will be used in assessing the performance of a project, which provide the illusion of accountability and the ability to measure results **3.** promised results that are conveniently written in the broadest and most vague language to ensure an interpretation indicating success, e.g., "We will obtain nationwide press coverage for Nougat Nuggets candy" is achieved via newspaper mentions in New York, Los Angeles, and Little Rock, Arkansas. ("Hey, is that not nationwide?")

deploy 1. to lay off **2.** one of the many sanitizing euphemisms for getting rid of people that companies insist on using even though everyone knows what it really means and finds the feeble attempt at linguistic camouflage insulting and even more evil than just saying "lay off" **3.** par-

ticularly offensive when used to refer to massive layoffs affecting thousands of people. *Synonyms:* downsize, let go, rightsize, smartsize. *See also* **merger.**

devil's advocate 1. one who adopts an opposing view in a nonpartisan way for the sake of testing an argument **2.** common **passive-aggressive** tactic for saying "I completely and totally disagree with you," e.g., "I think that's a viable strategy, but what if we tried my idea that is kind of the opposite of yours, just, you know, devil's advocate." *See also* **I don't disagree with that/I'm not opposed to that.**

dial it down/dial it back 1. to reduce intensity **2.** when used in reference to a person's behavior, to calm down or relax or get a freaking grip for God's sake; new-millennium version of "take a chill pill" or "chill out" **3.** when referring to a presentation or sales pitch, to be less aggressive in the hope the audience will not be aware they are being snowed with a soft sell. *See* **sales.**

difficult people 1. members of the workforce who are unpleasant to deal with **2.** Class A jerks of the workplace frequently found in the ranks of senior management **3.** common behavior includes temper tantrums, bullying, yelling, lying, being unnecessarily combative or uncooperative, backstabbing, undermining, manipulating, or just being plain batshit crazy. So prevalent that many companies will offer workshops on "Dealing with Difficult People," which aim to instruct employees on how to make day-to-day existence bearable through tactics that enable abusive personalities; **firing** these people never seems to be an option, as **HR** tends to turn a blind eye to what is deemed "unacceptable conduct" by those in **leadership** positions, even though the organization may have a policy of **zero tolerance** regarding abusive behavior.

dinner 1. a meal consumed in the evening hours **2.** the meal you can't get your company to pay for, even if you're working late and your plummeting blood sugar levels are dramatically affecting your ability to function; cheap takeout five nights straight at the office, which makes you feel like shit or get fat and is regarded more as "fuel" than food **3.** a business meal financed by the **boss**'s expense account, which usually involves a group of people who under normal circumstances would never break

bread together, and have nothing to say to each other, thereby creating a situation that would be really great—if your **friends** were there; senior employees will get loaded, junior employees will try to eat as much free food as they can without seeming gross, as their meager salaries subsidize only two meals a day **4.** a chance for the **boss** to expense a meal and claim that work was discussed, even though everyone knows they went out to dinner with their friends on the company dime **5.** an overrated **perk** that makes people feel hollow and lonely inside, as they have just pissed away three hours of their life gorging themselves with individuals they don't know or like; makes mac and cheese and a couple of 40s with college buddies seem wistfully sublime

direct report 1. the junior staffer in a supervisor/employee relationship **2.** a common term for the people "managed" by a particular person that underscores the senior person's power over the staffers, just in case they forget; will frequently be used in the possessive sense, i.e., "*My* direct reports" and may be irritatingly truncated to "My directs." *See also* **dotted line.**

disconnect 1. a misunderstanding; confusion relating to the communication of information **2.** as in "we had a disconnect"; a classic **CYA** move, as it implies unintentional error, but really means "I wasn't really listening to you, so that might explain why you didn't get what you asked for"; unless you screw up all the time, no one is going to call you on the carpet for this, as everyone has disconnects all the time. Valuable as a Get Out of Jail Free card. Also good for when you really do make a mistake but can't afford to acknowledge it **3.** can also be used aggressively by a senior employee to junior staffer, e.g., "We're having a disconnect," which is really a way of saying "You're stupid."/"Why can't you just get it through your thick skull what I'm telling you to do?"/"I don't think you understand that this is not up for discussion."/"Resistance is futile. Just do it." *See also* **miscommunication.**

diversity 1. a mix of many different kinds of people; heterogeneity in the workforce **2.** something many companies are deeply **committed** to in the form of companywide **initiatives,** which on the surface admirably seek to create an open, accepting, and **inclusive** work environment for people of different races, sexes, religions, sexual orientations, "able-bodiedness," etc.; some employees will deduce that the company has been threatened with or had to settle lawsuits, which served as a **wake-up call** that there might be a problem regarding these issues. **3.** such a basic, good, and obvious idea, and yet so mired in controversy and **office politics. Committees** will be convened to determine an organization's diversity **issues,** people will disagree on the priorities of the **initiative,** and **ass-kissers** will bend over backward to prove their **commitment** to the idea, treating it as just another **goal** linked to performance as opposed to actually internalizing the fundamental ideas of the effort. **4.** talk about a political hot potato! When diversity is in full effect, people will invoke its power to get anything done, e.g., "This is part of our work on the diversity **initiative." 5.** some people think it means "visible diversity" in the workplace, which some people think means "people of color" in the workplace, which some people think means "African-Americans or Latinos in the workforce," i.e., not Asians, which also leaves behind women, gays and lesbians, the handi-capped, etc., but somehow, *everybody* thinks serving food at the **cafeteria** that "represents" and "teaches" about different groups of people is a *great idea* (e.g., serving collard greens and jerk chicken during Black History Month, tacos and *churros* for Latino History Month, and lo mein and fortune cookies during Asian-Pacific Heritage Month). **6.** if your company launches a diversity **initiative** and is on fire about it, expect to see a token blind midget or a wheelchair-bound albino in the **cafeteria. 7.** ironically, companies that proclaim their unwavering, utmost dedication to making *all* employees feel valued and included through a diversity **initiative** only painfully underscore many employees' feelings of being undervalued and excluded, regardless of their race, color, creed, etc., especially the ones who have had a hand in creating, **marketing,** and distributing anything regarding the diversity **initiative,** the final message being "We are passionate about being open and inclusive to everyone, but just not to you, because everyone matters—but you."

divide and conquer 1. a strategy that involves distributing elements of a mission to separate parties as a way of increasing effectiveness and ensuring success **2.** a reference to strategy in an actual battle that is laughable in the context of a conference room, as most of the "warriors" are checking out Lisa's lace-trimmed camisole under her pinstripe jacket or trying to remember if Wednesday is baked ziti day at the **cafeteria 3.** division of tasks will always result in the **ass-kissers** attending to the mildly stimulating jobs or the **low-hanging fruit,** while the rest of the staff will be assigned the grunt/**busywork** that really needs to be done in order to get something accomplished, e.g., "Sheryl: You take the **clients** to **lunch** someplace nice and schmooze them. Sarah: **Touch base** with design and tell them our **time frame** has changed to next week, and make sure they deliver even though we don't have sign-off on the new **logo.** Steve: Pull all the projects we've worked on in the last five years and alphabetize them in reverse order so we can be **proactive** and have them ready the next time this happens. I'm going to be out of the office for the next few days, but I'll **circle back** with you when I return. Keep me posted. **Thanks.**"

doctor's appointment 1. a meeting with a health professional to receive medical care **2.** job **interview;** extremely oppressed/paranoid/smart employees will wear easily transformed outfits and duck into an ATM on the street à la a superhero to get interview-ready—those who don't will be met at the **office** with the comments "You look nice today!" and "What's the occasion?" from all. **3.** special escape hatch/loophole for women, particularly those with male **bosses,** is the inferred gynecologically related appointment, which essentially gives one a free pass plus one (for "complications") as no one, particularly a guy, is going to challenge you on the health of your cootchie **4.** **therapy** appointments present a problematic gray area, as these frequently require a late arrival/long **lunch** hour/early departure, and admitting that you have a doctor's appointment at 6:00 P.M. reads as "therapist" and labels you as "crazy" **5.** involves inherent injustice of staffers being instructed to schedule doctor's appointments in the predawn hours, or during **lunch,** while **managers** waltz in at 11:30 A.M. or leave for three hours at midday, citing "a doctor's appointment" as the cause for their absence

dog food 1. the term used to refer to a company's own product when it is tested within an organization before being released to the general marketplace **2.** a pretty nonambiguous term that indicates to employees how senior management feels about them

don't confuse a good story with fact 1. perception is reality **2.** if management believes something to be true, don't waste time trying to argue with information that does not support the idea, because it's **moving forward.**

don't pitch the bitch 1. an expression; do not attempt to sell to a woman. **2. sales** guy talk: don't bother trying to sell to the wife or female significant other, as they are high maintenance, difficult, fickle, and don't make the decisions in the household.

dotted line 1. refers to an uncodified or informal reporting situation on an **org chart 2.** you supervise an employee but are not given the **title,** money, credit, respect, etc., for doing so; a cost-effective strategy

download 1. to communicate information **2.** to relay information to junior staffers who will execute directives, or to other **colleagues** who are not present for a conversation **3.** basically a really annoying way of saying, "I'll *tell* them"; if said in regard to a staff, has a hint of "I am the master of my domain and I will pass this off to my legion of serfs, and they will make it so through the guidance of my supreme **leadership**"

drill down 1. to look at an issue in depth **2.** to do the work you said you were going to do in the first place, i.e., read it, investigate it, "get to the bottom of it," etc. **3.** a vaguely macho way of saying you'll research something, and the alliteration factor really drives it home **4.** term left over from the dot-com culture that refers to clicking a million links until you get what you want from a site, e.g., "How the hell do I talk to a customer service representative/a real living person if I want to?" *See also* **due diligence, vet.**

drink the Kool-Aid 1. to appropriate the thinking of the ruling class **2.** origin: Jim Jones's cult following, which resulted in people committing suicide en masse **3.** brainwashed; to have been a normal person who then starts using corporate bullshit, acts like nothing is wrong, and is using the language in this book and really, really likes management; if they still speak to you, will say, "They're really not that bad," or just clam up when going out for drinks (*beware:* they are moles) **4.** robot, pod person longing for the Third Reich who owns *Friends* on DVD; will become management, may have **smooth hair** and is definitely an **ass-kisser**

drinks 1. beverages **2.** alcoholic beverages **3.** if a bunch of employees go out for drinks, it means they are going to collectively get rip-roaring drunk, talk about how much they **hate** their **boss,** offer up juicy **office gossip** and **confidential** information **off the record,** and, depending on how smashed people get, some coworkers may go home together; one person will always end up puking in the **bathroom** or on the street. **4.** if an individual suggests that you get a drink with them after work, they are probably hoping that you'll both get rip-roaring drunk and then go home together. **5.** if the **boss** says he's taking everyone out for drinks, this is a trap devised to get employees so drunk on free booze that they'll spill their guts on topics they would never comment on while sober; the **outing** will be expensed on a **T&E** form as "**team**-building."

drug test 1. a diagnostic tool administered to determine if a subject has recently used an illicit chemical substance **2.** tool of the most draconian, top secret, and concerned (for good reason) workplaces, e.g., Wall Street firms, the CIA, and airlines, respectively; the threat of which gets prospective employees all in a tizzy—especially the ones who have been unemployed for eight months and have been sitting around smoking pot to take the edge off; also responsible for your usually pro-party **friend** gulping gallons of goldenseal-laced tea while declining a hit of whatever's being offered because they are awaiting an **interview** appointment with an employer that, sadly, never seems to arrive **3.** current employees may be subject to random drug tests, the corporate sister of jury duty; these are heralded by an out-of-the-blue call from **HR,** which most staffers learn to avoid/not pick up, or they are conveniently "traveling" when the request comes in. **4.** also source of cottage industry of wildly expensive quick-fix remedies for the chemically inclined, ranging from the herbal (detox teas) to the mechanical (battery-heated bags of clean piss), and earnest discussions in **Internet** chat rooms regarding the best ways to test negative, not to mention boring hysterics from straight arrows who believe they're not going to get a job because they ate a poppy-seed bagel. Also cornerstone of *High Times* ad revenue. **5.** of no concern to the SVP who reeks of schnapps at 11:00 A.M. and the EVP who fell down while heading to the **bathroom** at the last **client dinner**

due diligence 1. research **2.** to do one's homework, or actually learn the facts, details, etc., of a project; also known as—hello—doing one's job **3.** labor that results in **ass-kissers** or job candidates at **interviews** sprinkling random irrelevant factoids into conversation that not only disrupt the natural flow of discourse or business, but also make the person who's talking look like a giant geek **4.** work that is used to justify a negative assessment of a situation project, i.e., you'll hear plenty of people say things like, "I did the due diligence and it's just not cost-effective," but no one ever says, "I did the due diligence and it's a go! Full speed ahead!"

E

edgy 1. risky or provocative 2. often used in reference to **creative** content, indicating that it does not or should not immediately appear to be the work of a corporate institution. The subtext of this is, "but really, not. Like, we don't want to offend anyone," i.e., safe. Resulting work is watered down, vague, makes an outdated pop culture reference, or all of the above. **Creatives** who consistently produce genuinely thought-provoking work will ultimately either be pushed out or leave due to consistently negative **feedback,** negative press, and a perceived disregard for **diversity.**

eight-hundred-pound gorilla 1. a company that dominates an industry 2. a company that dominates an industry, annihilates even the remote possibility of competitors getting any considerable market share, and largely dictates the products available to consumers (i.e., theirs), all of which result in great frustration and hatred by everyone who doesn't work with or for them 3. Microsoft 4. the obvious problem or issue that everyone knows but doesn't discuss, usually due to the influence of **office politics,** i.e., **meetings** are held to improve **process,** but everyone knows that all the changes in the world can be made to **process,** but that doesn't change the fact that the **boss** won't ever make a decision; efforts to address how an application the company expended way too many resources on can be used more efficiently are pointless, because from the get-go it was a piece of junk, it's beyond fixing, and given the amount of resources it has consumed, it can't be trashed; evaluations of vendors are meaningless because the **boss** is having an **office romance** with one of the suppliers and it's already a lock, etc.

elevator etiquette 1. unspoken, socially dictated rules abided by when entering, exiting, or riding in an elevator **2.** code of conduct communicated through osmosis or by breathing the same air in a small mechanical box for minutes at a time; societal protocol includes men allowing women to exit and enter the elevator first and holding the door for them as they do so, pressing the "open door" button for someone racing to catch the elevator, avoiding using the elevator to go up or down one floor. **3.** behavioral guidelines that help make inhabiting a small box with strangers remotely possible, which include refraining from bitching or **gossiping** during a ride, or at the very least using code names or pronouns when discussing co-workers; pretending not to be listening to a juicy conversation should one occur; acting as if you don't see the **CEO** when he happens to board the car with you or refraining from telling him how screwed up everything is; making an effort to be subtle when checking out a person or their horrible/definitely not-appropriate-for-work outfit; riding the "close door" button to thwart others' efforts to board a car; ignoring the fact that someone just **farted,** big-time

elevator speech 1. a brief summary of the work one does, or of one's skills and ambitions, delivered during an elevator ride to another passenger, usually someone of greater importance and power **2.** refers to the short period of time one may spend in an elevator with a person more important than you/someone who can give you a job; **advocated** by people like guest speakers and **consultants** as a great way to get yourself noticed and make important connections. The reality is, this is not true, and in fact the delivery of an elevator speech may brand you as an annoying and intrusive person to be avoided at all costs. Anyone of importance who is trapped in an elevator with you is really hoping you don't try to bust out any of that elevator speech shit on them, because they just want to travel between floors in peace, and they know your idea sucks anyway. Plus, you're an idiot because you haven't figured out that the elevator speech is a bad idea.

e-mail 1. electronic mail; mode of communication via computer **2.** it is your **friend,** it is your enemy. It will comfort you, it will give you up. [*Please note:* If you don't know this already, many companies can access employees' e-mail files—yes, even the ones they've deleted. You don't have to send your note about your drunken one-night stand to the president to be totally **busted**.] **3.** The good: a lifeline to your friends that keeps you sane; source of random, slightly amusing pictures and annoying good luck charms (that despite your best instincts you fill out, wishing to get another job); great way to **CYA** by providing a written record of your efforts to do some work. The bad: as discussed, the whore that will sell you out; source of annoying work spam not conducive to getting work done when you actually need to do so; subject to digital politics such as the **cc** and the **bcc**. Reading work-related e-mail will invariably communicate to you where you rank on the evolutionary scale in your colleagues' eyes and cause you to contemplate jumping out an office window. **4.** it cannot be stressed enough that one should never send an e-mail without first rereading it and *making sure it is addressed to the intended recipients,* as you *will* write something to the effect that your **boss** is a tyrannical windbag who can go to hell, and . . . send it to them. Similarly, should

you receive an e-mail from a coworker that fills you with homicidal rage, *you must step away from the keyboard,* or you will compose an earth-scorching reply that, once sent, will become a permanent record of your **unprofessionalism.**

employee assistance program (EAP) 1. a company-sponsored program available to help the people who work for an organization get support regarding work and non–work related issues, and manage stress **2.** many EAPs will help you plan your wedding or adopt a pet (for real), but essentially, it's therapy-lite. There are counselors standing by at a 1–800 number for you to call if you're cracking under the stress and need someone to talk you off the metaphorical, or literal, ledge. Beyond a confidential chat with an anonymous person, EAP will also provide you with "short-term counseling" with one of their mental health professionals, which is, like, four sessions. As anyone who's "crazy" will tell you, a handful of chats with some random social worker is just not going to cut it, especially when you're tackling an issue like, "I'm a little concerned that I might have wasted my life, and I am often suffocated by deep despair." *See also* **therapy, antidepressant, crying.**

empower 1. to invest with ability or power **2.** self-helpy term that lots of managers and companies say they do to their employees. The problem is, being empowered means feeling in control and having the freedom to take action as determined by one's own judgment, which is kind of opposite of the effect that corporations seem **committed** to really driving home.

end run 1. an offensive play employed in the American game of football in which the ballcarrier attempts to run around one end of the defensive line **2.** an action, often born out of frustration and immediate need, that can get something done without going through the proper channels of approval, which everyone knows would take a million years **3.** if someone says, "We need to do an end run on this," they're asking, "Is there some way we can do this without the people who are supposed to know about it knowing about it?"

enterprise 1. a large company, particularly in the tech industry **2.** incredibly annoying word that serves to mystify a very simple concept: a business; people often use the phrase "across the enterprise," and all who do should be immediately beamed up or violently sucked into a rip in the fabric of the space-time continuum. **3.** usage is a way of letting people know you went to **Bschool.**

entitlement 1. the feeling that one is owed something **2.** the sense of deserving something—a promotion, a plum assignment, an **office**—without having done the work to get it, or through doing a mediocre job; signifies a lack of understanding of the rules of cause and effect; badge of honor for Generation Y **3.** expectations exhibited by employees who work for a company that provides **perks** that many others do not, which only serves to fuel worker demands for things like caffeine-free raspberry green tea, or an on-site gym, which employees at most companies wouldn't even dream of requesting. *See also* **Gen X/Gen Y interface.**

ergonomics 1. the field of equipment design geared toward reducing employee discomfort and potential physical injury such as repetitive stress disorder, with the goal of promoting worker productivity **2.** closest thing to a corporate spa, but "work-related," so it's legit; if you're lucky enough to work at a company that has a person whose job it is to ergonomically outfit your work space, go for it: They'll come by, assess your chair and its distance from your desk/phone, and order you cool stuff to make you more comfortable. If not, at the very least you can likely swing one of those squishy wrist rests for your keyboard and mouse, which are offered in lots of cool colors, feel really good, and during those slow moments provide a vaguely sensual pick-me-up due to their supple fleshlike response when squeezed (see the **office supplies** catalog for available options). **3.** excuse for ordering the wildly expensive Aeron chair, a symbolic artifact of the dot-com era—hey, if you can get one, why not? They're cool.

excellence 1. the state of being superior and without equal **2.** something many people and companies say they expect/ offer/won't accept anything but, that is revealed as being really cheap currency when you live on planet earth and observe the people who actually work at companies—like Brad, who still doesn't know how to transfer a call even though he's been an **administrative assistant** for two years; or Linda, who assaults her coworkers with visible grandma panty lines every day of the week; or Nick, the charming department head who **manages up** like a champ while things rot from the inside out **3.** a laughable hyperbole encouraged by **consultants,** gurus, and guest speakers **4.** in reality, the thing people should stop shooting for, because making things just kind of okay would be a really good start. Enough with the excellence and **perfection,** all right?

executive as _____ **1.** the identity of a senior person in an organization or department that is either created and encouraged by them or fashioned by those who work with them closely **a:** Executive as comedian: hallmarks include a suspiciously enormous amount of time spent doing what he or she believes to be entertaining or amusing to staffers, and acting "wacky" in the belief that their behavior will make them less intimidating to the worker bees; believe they improve morale by creating a "fun" and casual environment. Are, in fact, not in the least bit funny; those who adopt this persona are often frustrated professionally, having given up their dreams of being some kind of performer for a more comfortable corporate path. Abuse their authority by holding captive junior employees, who must feign enjoyment as a result of workplace power dynamic. Delusional and vaguely pathetic; have no idea that no one thinks they are funny **b:** executive as rock star: rooted in long past acts such as being in a punk band, crossing the Atlantic in a canoe, doing acid, attending Wesleyan, etc., which are hyped to obscure the exec's complete immersion in the corporate milieu and seven-figure salary. A mythical identity largely reserved for men, who may liberally curse or make drug references as a way of reinforcing their bad boy image; often have great hair and/or a hot wife **c:** executive as shivering bunny: counterintuitive to the fact that this person makes more money in a year than you will retire with, and the fact that they oversee dozens, hundreds, or indirectly even *thousands* of people, they are a mess—either desperately unsure, insecure, or para-noid—and need constant reassuring from those who are in their immediate orbit, be they assistants or SVPs of **corporate communications**. Drive everyone crazy; those who work for them spend more time babysitting them than doing the jobs they were actually hired to do. **d:** executive as Average Joe: perhaps the most insulting, the idea that the most highly compensated and powerful people in the company are "just like you," even though they have their own bathrooms, enormous penthouses and summer residences, go to dinner parties with Charlie Rose and Steve Martin, display Robert Rauschenberg's work in their homes, and could smite you with as little effort as batting an eyelid

executive decision 1. to independently make a definitive choice **2.** since most executives must secure sign-off from a litany of people and **committees** on even the smallest matter, this sure isn't happening in 98 percent of the company. **3.** organizations will pay much lip service to the idea of the **empowerment** of their employees, but should a staffer attempt to be **nimble** and actually make an executive decision, he will be severely reprimanded and labeled as impertinent or not **the right fit** for the company. *Also see* **making a decision by not making one.**

executive headshot 1. a professionally taken photo of a senior staffer, supplied to **trade publications** and consumer magazines by a company's **corporate communications** department or **PR people 2.** a photo of a senior person in the organization that looks nothing like them because it is several years old, airbrushed considerably, and features them smiling and/or looking like a nice and approachable person. *Note:* Execs will often get cosmetic surgery in the name of career advancement and bill it to the company. **3.** something it would be really awesome to have, because it would be great to use for your online dating profile

F

■■■■■■■■■■■■■■■■■■■■■■■■■■■■■■

facetime 1. time spent in the physical presence of someone. **2.** what is achieved when people kick it old school by actually dealing with someone in person; an annoying way of saying you'll be in the same room as your coworker, **client,** customer, etc., that has been given new life due to **telecommuting 3.** unnecessary hours logged at the office for the sole purpose of being seen and showing **commitment** to higher-ups, engaged in by **ass-kissers** who will just hang out until 8:00 P.M. if the **boss** is there, as if work is their favorite place in the world (sadly, this may be the case). **Bosses** love this, even though it could be a strong indicator of an inefficient employee, because they know on some level that the **ass-kisser** is sucking up to them, and it reinforces the idea that not having a life or people outside of work who care about you and might want to see you is normal. As a direct result, **office romances** may ensue. **4.** hours at the office that do not require doing any work, as just being there is enough, a fact that infuriates the employees who work hard all day to get things done so they can leave on time because they do have a life and people who care about them

facial hair 1. hair that grows on the face **2.** hair that typically grows on the faces of men, but, in some unfortunate cases, on the faces of women as well **3.** a prop that is groomed by men trying to appear hip, younger than they are, or, like, not so corporate, man; a joke that is painful for **colleagues** to endure, resulting in all sorts of ridiculous "expressions of style" such as elaborately pruned sideburns or the dreaded soulpatch, particularly by white guys (got that, daddy-o?)

fall down 1. to drop from an upright position, usually unintentionally **2.** a very, *very* nice way of saying "screw up"; most often used by people who are discussing their own errors, e.g., "Our execution of the WorkIsSuperGreat **initiative** was a home run, but admittedly, we really fell down when it came to the follow-through." In this context, people "fall" on several overstuffed feather beds wrapped in high-thread-count Egyptian cotton sheets, but it's worth pointing out that when people "fall down" in reality, it's often kind of violent, if not jarring, and most important, it's really, really hilarious.

family 1. a group of people related through blood or marriage **2.** overused metaphor, particularly in the nonprofit sector, describing a work environment, e.g., "like a family," "family atmosphere," "part of the family," etc. **3.** another way of saying "nobody makes any money here"; invocation of family bond ceases when it's time for layoffs.

famous people 1. individuals who are well known, often due to achievement or **talent** in a particular field or discipline **2.**

really overrated, annoying, often freaky people who despite their frequent high-maintenance and ridiculous behavior are criminally enabled by the countless weak souls they encounter, who are just so pumped to be able to drop the name of the celebrity they fetched water for into conversation with their friends who can't, they dispatch all standards they might have for assessing the value of a member of the human race **3.** cause of extremely uncomfortable dynamic in which everyone who encounters the famous person tries to act "really cool," as if the celebrity is not really that famous, while also offering to get down on all fours and serve as a personal ottoman for the noted individual should the need arise. If the reason a famous person is on hand is not immediately being attended to, there will be lots of standing around and uncomfortable faux casual conversation, as the nonfamous people in the room try to convince themselves they are "hanging out" with the famous person—which will also be referenced to friends not afforded the "opportunity" to do so. The famous person in question will be referred to as "really cool" in this context **4.** wherever famous people are, you can count on very young and "attractive" (read: made-up chicks in not exactly overtly sexy clothes/tan guys with bizarre **facial hair**/stupid jewelry) people somehow making their way onto the scene in an attempt to get their big break/get laid.

farm out 1. to contract work to an outside vendor, company, or individual **2.** to use money in the **budget** to hire someone to do something nobody wants to do; typically a really horrible or boring project. *Also see* **get a temp.**

fart 1. *slang*: an audible discharge of gas that in many instances may result in a foul odor **2.** despite being a socially unacceptable act, something many people have little shame doing at will in the workplace, to the point that it causes discomfort to their coworkers; **bosses**, capitalizing on their position of power, will often fart and expect no one to react, or in some cases may acknowledge their expulsion by saying "excuse me," as if they have not just grossed everyone out. **3.** one of the basic and most treasured advantages to having your own **office** (that no one talks about) is that you can fart whenever you want

to; however, farting with wild abandon will be punished by a **colleague** unexpectedly coming into your **office** immediately following the unleashing of a ripe one, resulting in deep shame and mutual uncomfortable denial of the diseased cloud floating around the room as you try to talk business.

feedback 1. information regarding one's performance on a project or overall **2.** information that can allegedly be positive or negative, but is always negative; may be presented as neutral information or as a favor ("Let me give you some feedback on this") **3.** a cornerstone of the **performance review** and cousin of **constructive criticism**

fire drill 1. a review of the procedures and actions to be taken in case of a fire **2.** typically biannual gathering of all the inhabitants on a floor during which the specifics of evacuation routes, stairwell fire doors, elevator mechanics, and the identities of the floor's **fire warden** and searchers are discussed; good opportunity to check out new blood on the floor **3.** traditionally avoided at all costs by employees, who will strategically have lunch or run errands when given advance notice that one is scheduled. However, in the aftermath of 9/11, attendance skyrocketed, and staffers who never attended one or usually checked out during them stood with rapt attention and asked alarmist questions about the building's air circulation; the truth is that 9/11 eliminated the need for fire drills, as everyone's policy now is to ignore instructions from the broadcast message system, hit the stairwells, and run like hell at the first sign of trouble. **4.** the longer you're at a job, the more frequently they seem to occur, even though they still happen only twice a year ("Didn't we just have one of these?"), thereby transforming the event into an extraordinarily depressing reference point that represents the cruel passage of time and your rapidly evaporating aspirations.

fire warden 1. a person who acts in an official and leadership position in the event of a fire **2.** Phyllis from legal, who not only seems to be volunteering for the position based on misguided, naked careerism, but who you wouldn't trust to put out a match in a monsoon **3.** assistants to fire wardens, known as "searchers," are charged with the task of making sure everyone is out of their **office** and accounted for, and come drill time may act as if they are principal cast members of the movie *Backdraft,* berating you until you come out for the **fire drill;** employees who feel they are too important to participate in the vulgar exercise of a **fire drill** will remain in their **offices,** dismissing the procedure altogether (the searchers will not look for them come towering inferno time).

fired 1. to have one's employment terminated due to negative circumstances **2.** your ass is canned. Much different from getting laid off, because you screwed up so bad they are ejecting you from the company **3.** what the hell did you do? Because the reality is, it's actually really kind of hard to get fired, because it's like taking a lit match to a can of gasoline: things can get explosive and lawsuits may crop up. When possible, many companies will buy out employees who have a history of **issues** at the organization (read: pay them for their silence), or just make someone's life so uncomfortable that they leave on their own.

first name basis 1. to have a relationship with someone who is familiar enough that you can call them by their first name **2.** referring to someone such as a **CEO** or **talent** by using only their first name, as if they are some sort of rock star (which to be fair, in the corporate world, they kind of are) à la Cher, Madonna, or Bono. Those who have met the person they are speaking of even once will refer to "Bill" or "Katie" or "Rupert" to imply that the person in question would know who the hell they were if they ever saw them again, or to just make those in the room who are not with the program think, "Wait, who is this Bill they're talking about? Is he in **accounts payable**?"; reinforces various **executive as** _____ myths, even though "Joe" could walk in the room and destroy everyone instantaneously, or be offered blow jobs by those who were just chatting about him like they were buddies **3.** when discussed on a first name basis, the person in question will always be "the most easygoing guy" or "so down-to-earth," even though the people talking about "George" have received a fierce secondhand ass-whipping as a direct result of his displeasure.

flowers 1. plants that produce blossoms, frequently given as a sign of affection or appreciation **2.** what you never get at the **office,** and what the annoying cute girl or the **CTNTSCWLWEL** with the loaded boyfriend always does, and then they reliably display them with a mix of smug embarrassment and pity **3.** what your **boss** also always gets, as an **ass-kissing thanks** for all the work you actually did on a successful project

focus group 1. a research tool that surveys a small group of consumers on their reaction to a product, with the goal of predicting the product's reception in the marketplace **2.** a group of people who are paid fifty bucks and a free lunch to measure the "likability" of a spokesperson, character, etc.; grade the subtleties of their preferences for multiple shades of orange, and determine if they would buy a cereal again or recommend it to a friend **3.** a group of people that a very select number of executives watch with rapt attention from behind a two-way mirror while eating lots of junk food; staffer access to focus groups is heavily guarded, as the fewer number of people who actually witness what the focus group says, the easier it will be to spin the results positively. **4.** any data from focus groups that does not support the feedback preferred by the people who are paying for the research will be discarded, guaranteeing positive support for the product being tested; following the completion of a round of focus groups, congratulatory **e-mails** declaring "overwhelming support" for the tested product will be distributed en masse. **5.** the sacred cow of research tools, which nonetheless frequently provides inaccurate information and ensures that Hollywood movie story lines will be saccharine and unsophisticated

follow-up 1. a discussion held after a meeting to discuss what transpired **2. a meeting** following the **pre-meet** and **meeting** associated with it **3.** depending on your work environment, will include people saying in really polite, modulated tones how someone blew it, or some obnoxious wannabe hotshot pointing out "fantasyland" fumbles and jockeying to take charge **4. meeting** held to discuss how a group is going to get the information they promised and perpetuate the elaborate myth they created in the **meeting.** *See also* **meeting.**

friends 1. people who are well liked by an individual **2.** people you contact to tell them they are going to do something for you—usually referred to as **reaching out**—whom you may or may not like; in fact, the relationship may be characterized by mutual animosity, but as long as the person **reaching out** has more power, they can say the two parties are friends.

functionality 1. the degree to which something enables its objective or task **2.** look: this is not a word. But basically, how something works, and how it helps someone do something, ideally what that someone wants it to do

FYI e-mail 1. an **e-mail** sent with the goal of making someone aware of a useful piece of information **2.** an **e-mail** that probably contains useful information that no one will read because "FYI" usually indicates extremely boring information is to follow; as a result, costly mistakes will occur. **3.** an **e-mail** you send to your **boss** to serve as evidence that you are working, or more often to give the impression you are working **4.** an **e-mail** sent to someone to **CYA;** will often include a **cc** or

bcc 5. a **nastygram** received with the alleged purpose of making you aware of a useful piece of information but is really a way of bitch-slapping you, telling you you screwed up, chipping away at your spirit; depending on the level of humiliation and public flogging the sender would like to inflict, may include a **cc**

G

gap analysis 1. the formal evaluation of the disparity between a desired performance goal and the current performance level 2. an official assessment of how badly something went wrong and how it got screwed up; also functions as a form of penance for those who have screwed up, who will ensure their **commitment** to making a thorough gap analysis to account for their sins, though they are probably hoping some other crisis will make everyone forget they're supposed to be doing one

Gen X/Gen Y interface 1. the workplace dynamic between employees who are members of Generation X with their younger **colleagues,** who are considered part of Generation Y 2. oil and water 3. Gen Xers, former latchkey kids infused with cynicism who entered the barren job market of the early nineties and took any position they could get, then scraped their way up to a passable living and a modicum of responsibility, were then charged with the duty of supervising a group whose every childhood whim was catered to, who got their first jobs in a flush economy that overcompensated new recruits, that is emboldened by an unearned sense of **entitlement** and confidence, and, to the Gen Xer, is annoyingly optimistic and ambitious; to Gen Y, their elders are uptight and bummers who won't let them do tasks reserved for vice presidents. 4. those of Gen Y are impatient that they are not given "real work" despite a lack of experience or skills; Gen Xers think their junior employees have no sense of paying their dues and are spoiled brats.

get a temp 1. an instruction to hire a **temp,** or temporary employee, for a short-term job or task 2. the quick solution to getting something done that no one wants to do, or to deal with the overwhelming backlog that results from staffers putting off doing something for months on end, e.g., filing a year's worth of **invoices,** cleaning out and organizing closets, data input, mass mailings, etc.

gift bag 1. a bag of free items given to guests of a function **2.** a bag of free stuff, AKA "swag bag," that will range widely in quality depending on the importance or prominence of the guests attending an event; examples include everything from high-end electronics, thousand-dollar sunglasses, and free spa treatments (reserved for celebrities) to leftover shampoo samples, a copy of a magazine, and Frisbees. **3.** primary reason for attending industry parties and **benefit dinners.** *See also* **premium.**

gift basket 1. a present, most often containing food, sent to thank a **client** for business **2.** slightly tacky cellophane-wrapped bribe to **kiss ass** and encourage future business, usually sent during the holidays; includes weird cheese spreads, crackers, shortbread, chocolate, assorted candies—all of which is placed in a public space for hun-

gry or rabid staffers to graze on, but only after management has raided them for the choice items; cheap gift baskets often take the form of pornographically large drums of flavored popcorn, which are addictive and proceed to make those who gorge on them sick—caramel, always the last to go, lingers until December 23. **3.** executive gift baskets, which contain booze, like champagne, are scurried away and will never be seen by the commoners.

Girl Scout cookies 1. small, sweet biscuits sold by members of Girl Scouts of the USA to raise funds **2.** what you will have no choice but to buy, because your **boss's kids,** or the **kids** of someone you're sucking up to, are selling them; some supervisors will ensure that no one can claim they didn't know the cookies were for sale by sending out a **mass e-mail** to the entire department announcing the news. **3.** reliable springtime source of empty calories in the form of Thin Mints, Trefoils, and Samoas, as at least one person will really go overboard with the **ass-kissing** and buy a dozen boxes **4. bosses** who do not push these will sell some other item such as wrapping paper, candles, etc., on behalf of their spawn

glass ceiling 1. *idiom*: the concept that women or minorities in the workplace are unable to achieve positions as high-ranking as the jobs held by their male counterparts, due to unacknowledged discrimination **2.** admittedly not as true as it used to be, however still largely applicable in the realm of a corporation's most senior management; women who do rise to positions of considerable authority are more likely to be found in the more "female-friendly" disciplines, such as **human resources, marketing,** and **PR** as opposed to **sales** or finance. **3.** in an effort to break the glass ceiling, some female executives may become **women who behave like men.**

goals 1. objectives **2.** objectives that are either thrust upon you by your **boss** or that you are forced to write yourself, which will very likely be used against you during your **performance review;** one way of trying to stack the odds in your favor is to write a set of goals that are really easy to achieve, but make them sound impressive through the use of vague language. For example, "Establish myself as the **team's** point person for all trade and industry-related information," which can be ticked off by reading a couple of **trade publications** and attending a **trade convention** or **conference,** or "Be an active contributor to the growth and development of junior staffers" can be accomplished by assigning some **interns** some **busywork,** sticking them in a **conference** room, and checking on them twice a day. *See also* **KPI.**

go-getter 1. a **proactive,** ambitious individual **2.** an irritating, obnoxious individual who invariably **drinks the Kool-Aid,** engages in **kissing ass,** and routinely attempts to take all of their coworkers' remotely interesting work **3.** the newest hire whose enthusiasm has yet to be crushed by their **boss** or the department's work environment, but will be after they realize they have done everyone's work for them and have nothing to show for it

go home! 1. a directive issued by a person in a position of authority instructing employees to leave work **2.** usually spoken by the **boss** in a friendly and encouraging tone in a moment when he is striking the "benevolent manager pose"—as he is walking out the door—to staffers toiling on a project that could not possibly be accomplished if said staffers left; if they were to leave and not produce the expected results, these employees would be met with a reprimand at a later date from a not-so-benevolent **boss,** who would admonish them for their poor **time management** skills. **3. ass-kissers/** those who have **drunk the Kool-Aid** will prance around the office like it's 10:00 A.M./they couldn't imagine a better place to be in the world and will in fact suggest doing more work, forcing you to seem like a bad apple/lazy person/not a **team player.** *See also* **facetime.**

going back to school 1. to leave the workplace to pursue a higher degree **2.** corporate-world experiment aborted: "Um, screw you people, I've had it. I'm outta here, to a place where I'll at least have possession of my own soul, and perhaps be able to get a better job when it's over. So long, suckas."

going forward 1. from now on, from this point forward. **2.** If someone is saying/writing this to you, you have probably screwed up. However, take heart, it is a benevolent phrase, implying, "Let's let bygones be bygones and we'll forget about it this time." But be forewarned, should you ever make the same mistake again, your foible will be dragged out from under the carpet and surely turn up on your **performance review** as an area for "improvement." *Also:* in the future . . .

going in a different direction 1. to deviate from a previously agreed-upon **goal 2.** a euphemism for "This exec is screwing things up and beyond help, even though he is doing what we told him to do. We need to bring in someone completely new to distance ourselves from that moron's [read: our] ideas and start from scratch. We're firing them to bring in fresh blood." *See also* **golden parachute** and **step down/resign.**

golden parachute 1. a compensation settlement received by a high-ranking executive such as a **CEO** when he is asked to leave a company **2.** an inconceivable amount of money and stocks given to someone who *did a bad job and is getting fired,* ensuring that neither they nor their descendants will ever have to work again. *See also* **going in a different direction.**

golf 1. a game played with clubs and a small, hard white ball on a large open course that has nine or eighteen holes; the object is to use as few club strokes as possible in the attempt to hit the ball into the hole **2.** a game previously the territory of rich, old, white senior management that now everybody has to play if they want a piece of the action; source of the constant queries "How's your game?" "Have you been out playing?" etc. **3.** gives rise to the slightly illogical and frustrating corporate axiom that having an excellent golf game will undoubtedly lead to professional success, due to the fact that skilled golfers will be asked to play with senior **colleagues,** fill in for others, and be remembered by upper management **4.** frequent pastime during off-hours at **offsites;** you can find those who have given up on the idea of being good at golf at the spa.

good-bye/retirement party 1. a festive gathering of people organized to express appreciation for a **colleague** who is leaving the company **2.** really boring and awkward affairs hovered over by the specter of disap-pointment and lost time, attended by scores of people who have never even spoken to the person who is leaving. The escapee can be identified by his giddy aura and a subtext of "See ya, wouldn't wanna be ya" to everything he says; some retirees may feel empty and depressed, as it hits them that they whittled away their lives in a soul-crushing job surrounded by people they hate. Coworkers attending the affair will be overcome with self-hatred, the feeling of being trapped, and an intense need for three more glasses of "celebratory" champagne. **3.** favored employees, regardless of length of time served, will receive more lavish send-offs that clearly communicate the inferiority and disposable nature of their coworkers.

gossip 1. informal talk of an intimate, confidential, or scandalous nature that has questionable sources and veracity **2.** a major currency of the workplace; careful purveyors of it will always have **friends,** as they are so fun to talk to and provide hours of entertainment in an extremely boring landscape **3.** unbelievable stories about coworkers that are too good or juicy to be true but that everyone takes as fact and repeats after *swearing* not to **4.** common topics include **office romances** and affairs, skeletons in exec's closets, behavior that required the **legal** department's involvement, and material that smacks of urban myth, e.g., "I heard that the executive vice president didn't know about 9/11 until 9/12." **5.** frequently completely baseless and false **6.** frequently entirely accurate

granular 1. of or relating to details **2.** almost always followed by the word "level"; implies getting down to the "nitty-gritty" or the heart of a matter, but ironically can be used to gloss over or avoid discussing specifics by simply referring to the granular level and moving on. *See also* **drill down.**

green 1. the color created by an equal mixing of yellow and blue hues **2.** very new or inexperienced; reference to young and new growth on **plants 3.** adjective used to describe young members of the workforce who are still idealistic and have no idea what they have gotten themselves into. *See also* **up is down, down is up** and **justice.**

growth opportunity 1. circumstance that offers the chance for someone or an organization to develop **2.** management spin for when something really sucky happens: you are put on an impossible project with a short deadline; you have a difficult **boss;** you are one of the few remaining people left after downsizing; you supervise a difficult employee

guesstimate 1. approximate appraisal **2.** a number, often regarding **time frame,** price, or **budget,** that frequently does not account for many of the factors that will affect the final figure **3.** those who offer a guesstimate will feel under no obligation to adhere to it, given the term's informal tone and the fact that its "root," after all, is the word "guess"; common tactic used to secure business, **buy-in,** or sign-off, by people who know that once a project is under way, it will be too late to back out, regardless of a misleading projection previously stated **4.** those who receive a guesstimate will lock it in as being entirely accurate, if not very close, and will never forget this number despite evidence and warnings to the contrary, ultimately resulting in complete shock and fury when a project is over **budget** or behind deadline.

H

harnessing intellectual capital
1. to identify the major strengths
of an organization and its employees and use this intelligence to the
greatest competitive advantage 2.
what senior management says
when it's run out of ideas on how
to fix a problem; good for at least
a few **off-sites** and six months of
stall time

hate 1. intense animosity 2. a
feeling you thought you had
given up a long time ago, as it's
an unsophisticated and juvenile
emotion more suited to a gram-
mar school—"hate is a strong
word"—and beneath a rational
and fully realized adult such as
yourself 3. something you feel
with deep, unmitigated, unwavering, and uncomplicated con-
viction toward whoever tortures
you at work (your **boss,** a particularly evil coworker, etc.), or
toward your job or company in
general, as it places you in an
environment of injustice, petty

power plays, and humiliation on
a daily basis. Will make you say
extremely venomous and strik-
ingly inspired things about people that in the past you might
have felt guilty about saying, but
now **celebrate** and take great
pleasure in expressing. Feels so
good.

have a good night 1. a phrase
instructing a person to enjoy the
remainder of their day 2. when
spoken by the **boss,** it officially
closes the end of the workday,
indicating that one is off the
hook regarding doing any more
real work; upon hearing this,
many employees will feel their
brains shut down and may find
themselves incapable of finish-
ing tasks regardless of workload
or deadlines 3. when spoken by
a **colleague** to someone still at
his desk, this can be roughly
translated to, "I am going to
have a good night because I am
leaving, while you will not be-

cause you are still here. Sucka." Other employees who hear this will be overcome by a feeling of being trapped, isolated, and, if the person walking out makes more money than them, fury and indignation. **4.** when spoken by staffers leaving the building together, this phrase, uttered at the threshold of the building or after immediately crossing it, is code for "this meaningless, seemingly interminable exchange of **small talk** is now over and I am entering my real life. I am no longer speaking to you and will now flee this awkward social situation like a bat out of hell. Don't even think about asking me which way I am walking."

help desk 1. the department within an organization that assists employees with the computers and software they use **2.** notoriously not helpful, and often destructive **3.** most people will avoid calling the help desk at all costs, as upon doing so, one enters a world of inefficiency and frustration; if an employee does call the help desk with a problem, the person they speak to will attempt to troubleshoot the issue over the phone, which means they will ask if the monitor is on or if the computer is plugged in. Upon

not solving the problem, they will invariably assign you a "job number" that is used to track your request and assure you that a member of their **team** is being dispatched to your desk, but will give you no sense of when that person will arrive. Frequently, by the time they do arrive, you will have given up and restarted your computer because you urgently need the document you're working on. If you have not done that by the time they arrive, they will show up, use a lot of tech speak to make it seem like they know what they're doing, and restart your computer for you, all the while making you feel the situation is somehow your fault. They will then disappear, possibly having wiped out your entire Outlook Express address book.

help me help you 1. a request so ridiculous it defies any attempt to actually define it **2.** a response from a **manager,** elicited by an employee who takes advantage of an **open door policy** and comes to him with a problem, which basically throws the issue back in the employee's face and says "Do my job for me" or "I don't have an answer for you," while also ignoring the fact that the employee came to the manager in the first place because he had run out of ideas to resolve a situation **3.** yet another attempt by **bosses** to force their employees, for their own good, to be problem-solvers, when it's really enough already; subtly implies that there's something wrong with the employee and ensures that a staff member will never take a problem to the **boss** again. *Also see* **open door policy.**

holiday halo effect 1. phenomenon that occurs in the days surrounding company-sanctioned time off in observance of a holiday, be it Christmas or Labor Day, that renders employees virtually unable to work; spurred on by many coworkers taking days off surrounding this time, resulting in significantly less-populated departments and the sense that no work is getting done anyway, so why work?; the principles of the holiday halo effect can also be applied to weekends (Mondays and Fridays are the least productive days of the week) and even single workdays (9:00 to 10:30 A.M. and 4:00 to 5:30 P.M. are spent gearing up and tuning out, respectively).

holiday party 1. a festive seasonal gathering held for the employees of a company at the end of the year **2.** events can range from the wildly extravagant (sushi stations, live music, rented venues, themed decorations, costumed attendants, taking a **company car** home, etc.) to the depressingly and insultingly meager (cheese and crackers from the in-house catering service, the assembly of staffers standing around in a **conference** room or lobby) **3.** regardless, many, many employees will get shitfaced drunk, late-evening confessions of how much people hate their **boss**/coworker/job will transpire, regrettable sexual liaisons will occur, and humiliating displays of "getting down" on the dance floor will ensue. It is not inconceivable that junior employees will do something that will follow them for the rest of their tenures at the company, like puking all over the **boss's** new coat, or very publicly making out with a guy from the **mail room. 4.** invariably, the more mild-mannered members of the organization will behave like maniacs while the more rambunctious personalities will look on in horror; prior to the event, female junior staffers will primp in the bathroom as if they are going to the prom or auditioning for *American Idol* and show

76

up tarted up or extremely over-dressed.

homophobia 1. the irrational fear of gay people **2.** one of the many attitudes that organizations have **zero tolerance** for, which, in fact, they do—and how! Because, you know, who's going to get upset by a gay joke every now and then? It's good stuff! **3.** even the most innocuous of **colleagues** may whip out a gay joke unexpectedly, causing their nonhomophobic co-workers, not to mention their *homosexual* coworkers, to internally recoil with horror and disgust; those employees who are tight with management, who are busy **championing** the **diversity initiative,** will avoid reprimand for their behavior. **4.** lesbians are subject to a particular form of homophobia in that they are not even fashionable in a *Queer Eye for the Straight Guy/Birdcage/*"Come into my office and let me tell you about my dating life" kind of way and are therefore rendered asexual or treated like Martians because they don't like guys, and that's just weird. Plus, straight men can't work a sexual tension vibe with them and as a result become very confused **5.** organizations with openly gay people in prominent positions will hold this up as an indicator of their **diverse** workplace; however, this does not do anything for the junior staffer in **sales** who oddly seems to have no personal life whatsoever.

HQ 1. *abbr* headquarters **2.** where all the important people work **3.** source of **merger** announcements and **layoffs 4.** location thought of by the people who don't work there as "the Death Star"

human resources (HR) 1. department responsible for staffing an organization, managing **benefits,** distributing information regarding company policies, addressing employee concerns, and resolving workplace conflicts **2.** the most **incompetent** department in any organization; completely ineffectual aside from notifying you, via **mass e-mail** or flyers, that you need to renew your health care elections **3.** big fans of the **open door policy;** will never, ever do anything about a poor/abusive/unethical work environment or situation unless it smells of a lawsuit, as they are completely in the pocket of senior management: worker bees are expendable, and senior talent doesn't like to hear that they are jerks or bad at their jobs. **4.**

really good at seeming sympathetic and concerned; will listen to you describe the horrors and frustrations of your workday for extended periods of time in the hope that your "letting off some steam" will quell your complaints; may give you **candy** during **meetings** in order to create a bonding experience **5.** by the nature of their jobs, perhaps the ultimate corporate drones and shills, a necessary evil created by the system to manage the "commodity" of people— really just there for the paycheck and benefits and five o'clock quitting time; the detritus of the corporate world, e.g., have you ever known anyone who wanted to be a human resources representative when they grew up? **6.** will sit silently in the **meeting** in which you are **fired**/laid off with a "Do I know you?" look on their face; are there in case you go "crazy," as if you couldn't take them out in a second, but whatever

hundo 1. *slang:* one hundred **2.** like "one hundred" is so hard to say. Dork.

I

I don't disagree with that/I'm not opposed to that 1. I am not against that **2.** spoken to a person in a position of authority such as a senior executive, **boss, client,** which really means, "I *do* disagree with that. It's a really stupid idea, but I have to be as deferential as possible when telling you why"; almost always followed by "but" **3.** can also be employed by **difficult people** who, even when they are agreeing with you on the simplest matter, can't bring themselves to say it

I hear you 1. *colloq:* "I understand what you are saying to me and its implications" **2.** a way of receiving angry or controversial sentiments in a faux compassionate manner laced with concern, that while vaguely social-worky, promises no action; many **managers** hope that just by "hearing" their employees, they will be able to quell discontent and avert conflict, having appeared to be open to receiving **feedback** or input from their employees. **3.** may be accompanied by an expression composed of squinted eyes and a slight frown as well as the reaching out to touch an employee's hand or arm to reinforce false empathy (which will make the employee think, "Please don't **touch** me"). *See also* **open door policy.**

I like people/I'm a people person 1. a phrase often uttered by extremely **green** job applicants who have no experience in the work world, as anyone who has spent time working has learned that most people are intolerable and annoying at best or just plain stupid at worst

ID 1. *abbr* identification, referring to an identification badge **2.** the piece of plastic given to you on your first day that enables you to get in and out of

79

your building. You will inevitably lose this, but still try not to, as the aggravation of not having your ID is profound, most noticeably in the scenario of when you are really late for an important **meeting** and the security guard who you see every morning and greets you with a smile suddenly has never seen you before and needs to call your **boss** so you can get into the building. **3.** a photographic record of what you looked like when you started working at the company; try not to look at it, because the "before" and "after" are not pretty.

if they don't like it, they can leave 1. the idea that unhappy employees are free to leave an organization at any time if they so choose **2.** subtext of all corporate policies, aimed at the anonymous throngs lower on the totem pole, even though the company's **talent** is its greatest resource **3.** so pervasive in companies with any kind of **prestige** or **brand** recognition, it might as well be printed on employee **IDs;** the message to employees is clear: not only do we not have to pay you competitively, you are expendable, and there are at least a thousand people out there right now who would love to

have your job, at half the salary. *Also see* **intern.**

impactful is not a word.

in a perfect world . . . 1. a phrase invoked to highlight less than ideal circumstances through the use of comparison to Utopia **2.** a nonconfrontational way of saying, "We can't/won't do that," as it implies, "We would if we could, and, in fact, we'd really like to." **3.** politically savvy form of **push back** when responding to a request from senior management that clearly indicates that they are completely out of touch with reality and how things really get done

in the loop 1. informed, i.e., "keep me in the loop" **2.** what loop, we have no idea, but hearing this brings no guarantee that you will be advised on the status of a project **3.** requesting to be kept in the loop is often an acknowledgment that you are about to be shut out by an employee and really just makes you look more pathetic. **4.** managers who are kept in the loop via **e-mails,** status **memos,** and voicemails will frequently ignore these communiqués until the near-conclusion of a project, at which point they will freak out, demand changes that require large amounts of money and man-hours, and accusingly ask why they were not made aware of the project's progression; will never take the fall and admit to their boss that they were completely checked out and unavailable. **5.** managers who are kept in the loop will ask employees, "Why are you telling me this?" or **e-mail** the response, "Please don't waste my time with details like this. It's importnat that you manage your work independently and take responsibility/**initiative.**"

in trouble 1. to be in a situation that results in reprimand or punishment **2.** amazingly, a term that full-grown adults who pay rent/mortgages, have a 401k plan, insurance, floss, etc., *and may even have children of their own* (who, by the way, actually do get "in trouble") use in the workplace; a sign of the infantilization of all who work in corporate culture; very sad, but common. Forgive yourself.

incentivize also not a word

inclusive 1. to be comprehensive in scope; to involve and embrace many people or ideas of varying types **2.** essentially, a word that caught on in corporate America because it just

sounds so damn good, and you can tack it on to **mission statements, initiatives,** comments on corporate **culture,** and so much more! But the truth is, the workplace is all about *exclusivity*—from the executives-only **meeting** regarding your department's restructuring, to the office **gossip** everyone but you knows, to the really awesome party/event/drinks with the high-profile **client** everybody but you went to. The truth is, exclusivity is the building block of the corporate workplace, because those who are "in" can feel better than those who are "out," and the higher on the food chain (i.e., **org chart**) you get, the more "included" you are and the better/more superior you can feel (that is, until your "really good **friend**" sells you out to get even higher on the food chain than you).

incompetence 1. complete inability to accomplish even the simplest of tasks **2.** oddly and apparently, one of the keys to achieving success in a corporate environment; those who exhibit extreme incompetence will inevitably supervise vast amounts of people and large departments, and will be extraordinarily well compensated for doing so; in the process they will make everyone who works for them crazy and extremely harried, as the staff will constantly be cleaning up the messes their incompetent **bosses** have created.

informational interview 1. a **meeting** with an experienced professional person, instigated by an individual who wishes to obtain a job in the senior person's field with the purpose of learning more about positions in the area and the industry overall **2.** for the experienced person, a real pain in the ass, perhaps committed to because the SVP of **sales'** daughter wants to get into publicity, or the experienced professional has a minute belief in karma and thinks it's the "right" thing to do (and frankly, could use the ego boost of someone thinking their job is really awesome)—either way, a total time-suck that gets rescheduled five times because it's of such low priority it's kind of off the radar **3.** for neophytes, a request for a job, even though they often show up ridiculously unprepared and with completely misinformed ideas about the industry being discussed; will often exude the aura of "so when are you going to give me/help me get a job?"

initiative, an 1. a company-wide program endorsed by senior management, often geared toward effecting qualitative and measurable **change** in organizational procedures or employee conduct **2.** when something is going so wrong in an organization (red tape is crippling even the simplest procedures; **sexual harassment** suits are cropping up right and left; turnover rate is alarmingly high; minority representation is token at best; all **managers** are completely inept at their jobs) that the problem finally bubbles up to the top, where it is determined that the **issue** threatens to affect the **bottom line**. Action will be taken in the form of an initiative, a multitiered program that will be **rolled out** with much fanfare in the form of **mass e-mails** and mail drops, posters, lip service from the **CEO** at the **town hall, Intranet** site postings, and the distribution of ugly free **premiums** emblazoned with the initiative's **logo** and slogan **3.** senior management execs may attend **off-sites** dedicated to the new program (the organization's way of saying, "It costs money to do this, so you know we're serious"), at which time they will be told how important the initiative is and get a chance to practice their serious face and exhibit commitment; employees who are appointed to any of the several **committees** created to address **issues** related to the initiative will be emboldened by their association with something **championed** by the **CEO** and expect everyone to drop anything they are doing in order to assist in related work. **4.** after a certain period of time determined by the nature of the initiative and the specific company where it was launched, it will go away and you'll never hear about it again, until it is reborn under another name a few years later.

initiative 1. taking action on one's own **2.** something junior employees will be told repeatedly by their **boss** to "take" or "show" and hear much about during their **performance review 3.** can also be roughly translated as "read my mind"; should a person attempt to take initiative, she will be rebuked for trying to cut corners, going behind her **boss's** back/not keeping him **in the loop,** not using common sense, trying to get away with something, or undermining the **boss's** authority.

innovative 1. ahead of the times; unlike what has come before **2.**

the same old material/product/ services, but recycled, and possibly **rebranded 3.** what the thing that went wrong was hailed as before it imploded and got the people who **championed,** signed-off on, or created it **fired**

input 1. information or thoughts that are contributed **2.** if something needs someone's input, that usually means, "We need to run this by Mr. SVP so he doesn't ream us when it comes out." It should be noted that even if an idea/document/ **e-mail** is flawless or laughably innocuous, Mr. SVP will be sure to take time out of his busy day to demand all kinds of changes if only to demonstrate his own power, or to make him feel, and remind others, that he is the one who calls the shots around the **office**. It is not uncommon for Mr. SVP to mandate massive unnecessary changes that cost huge amounts of time and money, cause his staff to run around in a perpetually panicked state, and turn an otherwise simple task into a crisis.

institutional knowledge 1. information about a company, usually gained through a long tenure there **2.** awareness of where the bodies are buried and how they got there; may be a factor in obtaining job security **3.** the employee who possesses institutional knowledge will be the person everyone comes to when they have a question, because this is the only person who was around when anything happened, or is the only person who remembers it; this insider might also have files pertaining to it on a hard drive, but is the only one who would know what they are named. All of this will make the employee irreplaceable. *Also see* **old person.**

interesting 1. to arouse curiosity **2.** due to its vague nature, open to multiple interpretations; an ostensibly safe and neutral way of commenting on something; essentially a way of providing an opinion on a topic without really giving one **3.** used to express "that's really stupid" without paying any of the potential consequences of actually saying so **4.** a noncommittal comment, useful in that it has no implications of taking any action regarding the information provided, e.g., "That's an interesting idea . . ." **5.** code for scandalous or illegal activity; "You may find the accounting procedures interesting."

interface verbally 1. to speak to someone **2.** most often used af-

ter a series of **e-mail** exchanges, possibly including a **nastygram,** have grown contentious, e.g., "If you would like to interface verbally about this, I will be in all day tomorrow. Please feel free to give me a call at any time. **Best personal regards.**" **3.** essentially, "I will meet you on the phone at dawn and we'll have a shootout. Bitch."

intern 1. a person, most often of college age or a recent graduate, working for no or low wages in exchange for the experience of familiarizing themselves with a work environment or industry **2.** free labor, referred to by hardened staffers as "slaves" and subject to humiliation and lascivious comments from said staffers, unbeknownst to them **3.** young, nubile influx to **office** buildings, most noticeable by the roving packs that appear in early fall, spring, and summer; instantly identifiable by their palpable and oppressively inappropriate excitement regarding any task. **4.** desperate for a job, indicated by gaze of severe commitment when fielding a request for copies or **coffee;** may bring only the appearance of this commitment to a duty and completely screw up what you asked them to do, thereby making your job more difficult—the precise opposite of their purpose **5.** the most annoying specimen will be chummy with your **boss,** expect to take over the duties and assignments you have worked a decade or so for the "privilege" of having, and, in fact, will think you should be **fired** and they should get your job. Grim reminder of you in your youth, when you had hope, energy, promise, and a physique reasonably attractive to potential suitors. *Also see* **Gen X/Gen Y interface.**

Internet 1. a worldwide system of interconnected networks accessed through an electronic device, most often a computer **2.** very much like **e-mail,** a blessing and a curse, but mostly a blessing as it provides an almost infinite amount of options in the effort to avoid work, including online dating, shopping, reading or updating **blogs,** aimlessly surfing, managing your stock portfolio, looking for real estate, checking your nontraceable **e-mail** account, looking at porn (not advised), stalking exes and their current boyfriend/girlfriend, and, of course, looking and applying for jobs. Really: what did people do before the Internet—work? **3.** may be problematic in a variety of ways in that excessive use of the Internet for non–work related

purposes is frowned upon, and you will inevitably get **busted** by your **boss,** even if you are the quickest click in the West when it comes to closing browser windows; additionally, a leisurely surfing break intended to last fifteen minutes can easily morph into an entire afternoon suddenly gone, and before long you've lost many months of your life that you can't account for and have nothing to show for. *Also see* **Internet usage policy.**

Internet usage policy 1. a set of rules, as determined by a company, dictating employees' acceptable use of the **Internet** while at work **2.** every company has one, and you probably got it via a **mass e-mail** and deleted it instantly. What they say, in a nutshell: don't use the **Internet** for anything that is not pertinent to your job. What that means: no eBay, no checking your Hotmail account, no Gawker.com, no Kazaa or Limewire, no updating your **blog,** no online gambling, no **Internet** dating, and, yes, no porn. Essentially, no fun **3.** of course, companies know that everyone is surfing the Web all the time, but these policies exist as a way for them to **bust** you for something should they need or want to; some companies actually spot-monitor **Internet** use, others will just check out where you've been online if you've been placed on their radar for some reason (yes, as is the case with **e-mail**, they can do this); **micromanagers** will see it as their personal mission to **bust** you for surfing the Web, but that's not company-mandated, it's just a product of them being petty and obsessive control freaks with nothing better to do. **4.** still, it's not a good idea to look at porn at work

interview 1. a conversation with a job candidate conducted by a potential employer, used to evaluate the prospective employee's qualifications for a position **2.** a riddle wrapped in an enigma shrouded in mystery, with a heavy dusting of stress and anxiety, the sure sense that you are going to blow it, and an unprecedented tidal wave of sweat à la Albert Brooks in the film *Broadcast News* **3.** root of infinite attempts to crack the code of what **HR** people and hiring **managers** want, and neurotic attempts of desperate applicants to present themselves as "the one," e.g., suit or separates?; needlessly memorizing the company's annual report or Web site at one in the morning; spending copious amounts of money on new clothes, manicures, shoes, portfolios; analyzing the correct balance between confidence and deference or familiarity and formality; obsessing over whether to wait to be offered a seat or just take one, the science of the perfect handshake, etc. **4.** an evaluative conversation heavily weighted in favor of the person conducting it, who may be very qualified and knows everything about the job being offered (the **boss**) or who may have no clue what the job is (**human resources** staffer functioning as a "weed out the freaks and morons" screen); forum for familiar, sometimes trite questions such as "Where do you want to be in five years?" "What do you consider your weaknesses?" "Why did you leave/do you want to leave X company?"; the irony is that an interview is held to hopefully get an accurate sense of a job candidate, and yet the real truth, such as "I really want to be a caterer," "I have no organizational skills and I find files by sort of 'feeling' where they are, which sometimes works and sometimes doesn't," and "I left because I **hated/hate** my **boss**" can never be spoken, even though everyone knows what's being said is not the whole story, and the interviewers themselves want to start a scuba diving school in Venezuela/have a fear of public speaking/left because they had an **office romance** at their old job and had to get the hell out. **5.** a complete mindfuck that defies all logic: the interview you think you aced and that produced an offer of a second meeting with higher-ups will be followed by deafening silence despite multiple follow-up calls and **e-mails**; the one you phoned in while hung over will produce a job offer. **6.** forum for potential torture by hiring **managers** who have a sadistic bent and will unconsciously project all of their neuroses onto a candidate and get off on the inherently imbalanced power dynamic **7.** technique for weeding out competent and therefore threatening job candidates. *Also see* **résumé, the right fit.**

Intranet 1. an internal network site available exclusively to employees of an organization, used to communicate company news and provide access to business-related information **2.** looks like a Web site, if it was designed in 1981; extraordinarily difficult to navigate, bloated with useless information masterminded by the **corporate** **communications** department, but good for finding someone's phone number and the **cafeteria** menu; may offer an employee bulletin board that is helpful for scoring apartments, used furniture, and the occasional concert ticket, but it's also the forum for inane debates on the topics of the latest pop culture phenomenon (*Star Wars* movie adaptations, *The Apprentice, Extreme Makeover,* etc.), which serve as an outlet for employees who want a job in which they can express their opinions and exert influence, but instead become known as "that person who is weirdly and deeply invested in the Intranet chat forum—by the way, does he do any work?"

invisible 1. not able to be seen **2.** what you will become when someone you know is around you but does not want to be associated with you, usually because they are **kissing the ass** of someone more important nearby; can be extremely shocking, disturbing, and, sometimes, embarrassing if you happen to start to say hello to them and they walk right by you like you're in a corporate-themed *A Christmas Carol* or an episode of *Bewitched;* not uncommon for the **boss** to suddenly render you invisible **3.** mutual invisibility occurs when two parties make an unspoken agreement to not see each other, such as when you still run into someone you briefly dealt with three years before, and neither of you can muster the energy to say "hi" to each other anymore

invoice 1. a bill **2.** that's it: a bill. Will often be past due, not paid, etc., a situation you will have to deal with if you are **support staff** or an **administrative assistant**

issue 1. something in question **2.** a wimpy way of saying there's a problem, even though everyone knows an issue means there's a problem; people will "have issue" and "take issue" with things, which is slightly more aggressive, as it sounds like something someone on a debate team would say.

it is what it is 1. something is what it is **2.** empty statement; used when there is nothing to say about something, or when a situation is so screwed up it's not worth making an effort to fix it. Not unlike **at the end of the day** in that it masquerades as being somewhat definitive in an almost comforting way and just sounds good

it takes as long as the amount of time you have 1. a corporate axiom regarding the time one is given to do a task and the time it will take to complete it **2.** simply put: if you have two days to accomplish three tasks, it will take two days to get them done; if you have the same two days to accomplish twelve tasks, you will accomplish them in that time. If you are regularly given few things to do, you may find it incredibly difficult to do any of them regardless of how simple the tasks are and may, in fact, miss deadlines due to extreme lethargy; contributor to gross inefficiency.

it's not brain surgery/rocket science 1. an expression used to convey the simple nature of something **2.** a tired statement of the obvious, because even if something is pretty complicated, it's still not neurosurgery **3.** can be employed to intentionally mislead someone, like a new trainee, who is being given a near-impossible task that many who have gone before them have failed to accomplish **4.** um . . . *rocket?* do these people live in 1950/Fisher-Price land? *Also see* **we're not curing cancer.**

I've heard . . . 1. *contr*: I have heard; I have been informed **2.**

what **managers** say to you when they want to scold you for something but don't have the balls to admit it, either because they are wimps, are trying to shift responsibility, or are trying to make you paranoid; implies that other people have mentioned or complained about your behavior or actions to your supervisor, but when you speak to anyone who may have even remotely done so (your coworkers), they express confusion and laugh about the completely absurd idea of saying anything about the allegedly offensive action, i.e., it's not true. *Also known as* someone mentioned to me/people have noticed

J

juice baiting 1. to gain an employee's trust or knowledge of a situation by discussing privileged work or coworker-related information 2. a tactic used by a **boss** to make an employee feel special, more trustworthy, or just better than their coworkers with the goal of manipulating them into disclosing information that is being kept from the supervisor; any resulting sense of privilege or closeness will be neutralized by harsh coworker criticism or ridicule of the junior employee, or the **cold shoulder 3.** may also take the form of a **manager** remarking, "Did you see Joan in those stretch pants?" To which you *should* reply, "No, I didn't notice." However, instead you say, "Yeah, she looked like a stuffed sausage casing" and instantly realize that your despised **boss** now has the upper hand, even more than before, because you know that he or she will probably let it slip to Joan that you think she's a fat pig.

just so you know 1. a conversational introductory phrase indicating a minor, but perhaps helpful piece of information 2. classic **passive-aggressive** move; you're being helped—but not really. If someone says this to you, expect to be immediately informed of how something you did is not correct, approved of, "the way things are done around here," etc., commonly spoken to new employees who have not yet incorporated the dysfunctional and completely illogical mores of their new workplace 3. standard trope employed by **managers** in a spineless effort to reprimand employees while also trying to not seem like the "bad guy," usually because what they're **calling out** is absurd and they don't want to be challenged for pointing out the "infraction" 4. also commonly employed by **office** rivals who act real friendly to your face, but want you to know you're going down, e.g., "Just so you know, when I had

lunch with [our **boss**] last week, she mentioned that she was concerned about your area's responsiveness. I totally had your back, but I wasn't sure what to say . . ."

justice 1. moral rightness **2.** a principle dictating that those who do wrong will be punished, and those who do good will be rewarded and recognized **3.** let it go, not applicable, "lose all hope ye who enter here," etc. Those employees who expect this will be regarded and dismissed as being naive and **green**. *See also* **up is down, down is up.**

K

....

kick the tires 1. to get down to work **2.** a phrase invoked when work really needs to be done, whether because a project has been put off for too long or the **client** is expecting the completion of a job by a certain deadline

kids 1. children **2.** very small people who have no place in the cruel adult world of work and therefore seem like aliens or an apparition when you see them walking down the hall in their noticeably, and impossibly, tiny and cute shoes **3.** no matter whose kids are in the **office,** most people will fawn over them and talk like a moron to the children, and tell the parent how cute her offspring are, ignoring the fact that, just by the law of averages, there are some really ugly kids out there and somebody at work has one; kids of execs will get more attention and, often, presents. They will also be wearing clothing that retails for more than the cost of your entire outfit.

kissing ass 1. to seek the favor of an individual, most frequently a person in a position of authority, through flattery and general sycophantic behavior **2.** the number one way to get ahead in an organization, far outweighing other efforts such as working hard or working well. **3.** practitioners of ass-kissing engage in heavy amounts of **facetime,** shamelessly enable the **executive as comedian** with raucous laughter, and will offer to help with your projects if the **boss** is within earshot. If attractive, may safely flirt with higher-ups. Could very well be the laziest person in the **office** and will so get promoted before you. *Also known as* brown-nosing, a reference to the "ass" part of **kissing ass,** that you're smart enough to figure out on your own

KPI 1. *acronym* Key Performance Indicator; a metric/standard used for measuring the progress of an organization or employee against stated **goals 2.** an aid to determining exactly how badly you're doing

L

labor arbitrage 1. a cost-saving strategy applied to workforce management 2. taking all the jobs of a company and moving them overseas to increase **ROI;** highly sanitized phrase for "those people are toast"

lateral move 1. a **change** in jobs that maintains an employee's current salary and **title 2.** a sign that someone hated their job so much that the chance to get the hell out was infinitely more seductive than a potential opportunity offering more pay and seniority, if the latter meant spending one more week in the employee's current professional circumstances **3.** a hit that **pigeonholed** employees take in an effort to move from one field to another, knowing that in fact they could wind up reporting to someone ten years their junior **4.** when an employee is transferred to another position within an organization from a job in

which they were subject to abusive or inappropriate behavior by a supervisor; an escape hatch for both the employee, who has most likely lodged complaints against the **manager,** and the company, which is trying to avoid a lawsuit by shuffling the person out of harm's way

leadership 1. guidance or direction commonly provided to a large group by a person or small group of people 2. a phenomenon that requires decisiveness, **vision,** the ability to be articulate, and, in an ideal **world,** integrity (but who are we kidding?), which explains why it is virtually nonexistent in corporate America; some executives may confuse yelling, or being completely impossible to get an answer out of, for leadership **3.** a fancy, dressed-up way of saying management; companies that launch leadership **initiatives** after having discovered a management crisis across the **enterprise** will trot this word out, imbuing the program's focus with nobility, grandeur, and hyperbole, to which employees' reactions will be, "Shit. I'm not looking for Nelson Mandela or Martin Luther King Jr., just give me a **manager** who acknowledges my work, treats me fairly, and doesn't tell me when I can go to the **bathroom**."

legal 1. department responsible for all things related to the law, including negotiations relating to employment, rights, and contracts as well as any legal action taken against a company **2.** the in-house lawyers, who have a permanent poopy-face/ inferiority complex because they feel everyone sees them as necessary evils, nitpickers, and uptight stuffed shirts, even though they get paid tons of cash to be that way and are the ones who decided to kiss their psychology degree good-bye and go to law school in the first place—in the interest of making tons of cash **3.** the real **human resources** department when it comes to solving problems. If you've got a complaint (about, say, **sexual harassment,** discrimination of any kind, or abusive management) and legal gets involved,

now you're talking turkey, as it means they're really listening—because they think you might be able to sue them. Otherwise, you'll be stuck talking to the highly unhelpful folks in **HR.** If you meet with legal, think transfer or payout **4.** part of the corporate machine who, like the metallic dude in *Terminator 2*, will just keep coming at you, because they're on salary, and they work fifty hours a week to constantly fax and mail threatening letters. It's their job, and they're well funded: be afraid; be very afraid.

legs 1. *slang*: as in "to have legs"; a quality that will enable something to move forward or progress **2.** used to describe an idea, proposal, deal, etc., that, unlike most ideas, proposals, or deals, may actually go somewhere, usually because it has, or is likely to get, management **buy-in 3.** code for "We can spin this so we can get management **buy-in.**"

let me know your thoughts 1. a request for input **2.** common close to **e-mails;** in reality, not a request for feedback, but a veiled solicitation of support. Should not be responded to unless you are in complete agreement with the subject being discussed

leverage 1. to accentuate and use to the greatest advantage when attempting to accomplish something **2.** to hype the strengths of an organization, plan, or business partnership to fool people into thinking that what is being offered is better or more desirable than it really is; anything, particularly intangibles, can be leveraged: **talent,** resources, global networks, relationships, **brands** or brand recognition, etc. **3.** much like **paradigm** and **synergy** (*Note:* people will often speak of "leveraging **synergy**"), a word that is spoken far too frequently and is at best only vaguely understood by all who deliver and hear it; will also be used to make others in the room feel stupid or to make a presentation seem impressive and worthy of **buy-in**

Lite FM™ 1. nationally syndicated radio format featuring easy listening and adult contemporary songs **2.** ostensibly the least offensive choice of music (read: safe); however, in reality, Chinese water torture is easier to endure. **3.** choice of **receptionists** everywhere; woe to the person who shares an office/cubicle space with the person who controls the radio and favors the Lite FM™ format **4.** radio format that plays the same songs all day every day, and has been for the last twenty years, while padding the bank accounts of artists such as Lionel Richie, Sade, Air Supply, and Chicago; favored compositions—far too many to mention—include Carole King's "It's Too Late," Daryl Hall and John Oates's "Sara Smile," Cyndi Lauper's "Time after Time," Billy Joel's "Tell Her About It," and Joe Cocker and Jennifer Warnes's "Up Where We Belong."

living document 1. a document that is continually updated and revised according to new information relevant to its contents, with the goal of maintaining its accuracy **2.** a document that is supposed to be continually updated and revised according to new information relevant to its contents, but isn't—either updated, or accurate **3.** a document that has been created in an attempt to make sure everyone is **on the same page,** because somebody made a big mistake when they **moved forward,** acting on the assumption that they had the most current information. Is never accurate for a multitude of reasons: people forget to update it, the person responsible for maintaining it is not given new information, the server hosting it constantly crashes, a few differing versions somehow start floating around, or people blow off updating it because that's **busywork.** The well-intentioned soul who sets aside information to add at a later date will be entering outdated material by the time they actually get around to doing it, further ensuring the document's inaccuracy.

logo 1. a trademarked symbol used to represent a company, ideally embodying its function and identity **2.** the graphic representation of a company, which is usually just the name of the company written in a specific font of a specific Pantone color; something **marketing** people get really hyper about if it doesn't adhere to (AKA "isn't compliant" with) the style guide, the bible of how the logo may be used **3.** a sometimes indecipherable graphic or illustration that communicates absolutely nothing about the company, including what the hell it does; at times, this is intentional, e.g., the Altria logo, the British Petroleum logo. *See also* **brand, brand refresh.**

low-hanging fruit 1. something easily attained or accomplished; often used regarding potential customers in a **sales** context, but may also refer to **goals, deliverables, KPI,** etc. **2.** something that's easy to do; without it, the **pipeline** would be empty.

lunch 1. midday meal **2.** the company-sanctioned period during which you are allowed to leave the building in the name of eating food, but often don't and instead eat in front of your computer out of a cardboard box provided by the **cafeteria 3.** if someone asks you to "lunch," they could want any number of things: to pump you for information; talk to you in the hope you can give them a job; talk to you in the hope they can hire you away from your current employer; create a friendly relationship with you that will serve them in the arena of **office politics**/create an alliance with you so that they can screw someone else or just bitch **off the record.**

M

....

mail room 1. center dedicated to receiving, processing, and distributing an organization's mail **2.** notorious for being a black hole, particularly for extremely important FedEx packages scheduled for an early A.M. delivery; apprehending such an item will necessitate making several calls regarding the package's whereabouts and, ultimately, physically going to the mail room—once there, an employee seeking an item will either see it sitting in plain sight or be told it has been lost. **3.** stark space lit with fluorescent lights that usually looks like a category 4 hurricane has just passed through; may be filled with mood music ranging from very loud hard rock to hip-hop **4.** source of some of the company's nicest and most helpful employees, the people who physically deliver the mail to each floor

making a decision by not making one 1. to provide an answer through the act of not providing one **2.** extremely common and passive phenomenon/tactic employed by senior **managers** who are allegedly in their positions in part because of their ability to make smart decisions, let alone *any decision at all* **3.** cause of employees incessantly **checking in,** covering, and anticipating as well as countless hours of labor preparing for multiple outcomes due to the fact that a definitive one is yet to be determined **4.** once a decision has officially not been made (i.e., a **deadline** has passed), staffers will be expected to work **overtime** in an effort to meet the **goals** of the scenario created by the decision not made **5.** source of overwhelming inefficiency, an approach that management claims to be **committed** to reducing

manage up 1. to place the needs, both immediate and long term, of a supervisor above all other concerns, with the **goal** of ensuring the **boss's** approval **2.** all about putting on a good show; the department can be falling apart, but if the **boss** is happy, it's all good; a common root of neglectful and irresponsible management, because supervising a staff is too much trouble when you have your head up the **boss's** ass, and if you're managing up well, it won't matter what's going on with your employees anyway. **3.** if protracted, may result in really ugly secrets involving abusive management, **sexual harassment,** and creative accounting eventually coming out, all of which occurred while someone was not minding the store. *Also see* **kissing ass, perception.**

management tone 1. a tenor used by people in a senior position **2.** an annoying vocal affectation that is very transparent and laughable/repugnant to everyone who encounters it, that **managers** adopt when addressing "the little people" or a large group; will vary depending on the audience and the circumstances of delivery **3.** when reprimanding an employee for a minor infraction, a **manager** will often adopt a casual tone, or one that sounds as if he is making a request, even though

the issue being discussed is nonnegotiable. **4.** when speaking to a group, many **managers** will speak in soft, modulated tones that are meant to convey sincerity, but in fact do just the opposite. This variable is commonly used by women execs and/or in remarks being made by anyone expressing appreciation for "all the work you do"— even though the speaker doesn't have the foggiest idea what that work is, and how, on a daily basis, they are directly responsible for making it harder to get it done.

management training 1. company-sponsored instructional sessions held with the purpose of teaching employees in supervisory positions how to be effective **managers 2.** half-day seminars delivered by **consultants** or members of the in-house development staff that present a pie-in-the-sky ideal of how to effectively manage people; may include participants listing the qualities they have most and least admired in **managers** they have worked for, **roleplaying,** discussions on dealing with **difficult** employees, taking a **Myers-Briggs** test or identifying one's "style," a reminder of what's illegal (read: "Don't do this or we'll be sued"), suggestions for delivering **feedback** or on how to **fire** someone and on conducting a **performance review 3.** waste of time and of the binder full of paper trainees walk away with, as most managers learn from or are beholden to their own **manager's** style, rules, and whims, and even if they wanted to, they could not execute the behaviors and actions recommended in these classes **4.** logically, it follows that employees will note a marked discrepancy between the **manager** they are allegedly being trained to be, and their own **5.** attending this is an easy way to meet a **goal,** as it requires only showing up and pretending to pay attention, and often even involves getting a free **lunch,** including cookies, the high-end soft kind with the square chocolate chunks— bonus!

manager 1. individual whose responsibility it is to oversee and evaluate the work of others **2.** God help these people; it would appear that the main qualification for being a manager is to have absolutely no qualifications or aptitude for managing anyone, or, more to the point, to have the ability to really excel at sucking at managing people. Managers can be identified by their overall **incompetence,** which manifests itself in infinite ways. For example: having no knowledge of how the jobs of the people they supervise are actually done; a complete inability to handle stress; a propensity to use humiliation/guilt/manipulation/screaming as a "motivational tool"; a healthy dose of self-delusion that inhibits their ability to see that they are committing the very same acts they admonish and penalize their employees for doing, and the impact that might have on **morale;** an inability to relate to people like a normal person, especially when delivering less-than-positive **feedback;** overall evasiveness and cloak-and-dagger secrecy; general laziness; self-absorption, psychopathic, or antisocial personality tendencies that are identified in the DSM-IV (for real: check it out); etc., etc., etc. The irony, of course, is that your manager gets paid a lot more than you do, to "manage" you. And the fact is, on top of making your life hell, you may spend a good part of your workday managing your manager (which will, of course, ultimately result in your manager informing you that you need to work on your **time management** skills in your **performance review). 3.**

senior management is catching on to the management "crisis" (see above definition as well as the empirical data of people fleeing departments in droves, AKA "turnover"), evidenced by the institution of assorted management **initiatives** and **management training** programs, which entrenched, bad managers don't attend most of the time, and, if they do, it's so they can check off one of their **goals** and get their **bonus,** so they don't really pay attention to anything that's being said. *See also* **boss, manage up, management training.**

marketing 1. the presentation and positioning of a product or service with the goal of making sales to consumers **2.** marketing professionals are the snake oil salesmen of business, even more so than the actual **sales** people. They prey on consumers' hopes, desires, dreams, and the frequently false notions of who people they think they are, or want to be; marketers encourage consumers to believe they can *buy* who they are. **3.** marketing is why people buy four-dollar caffeinated drinks, wear T-shirts emblazoned with company names and **logos** (i.e., *a walking advertisement—for free*), and feel safe/secure/in the know/

better than everyone else shopping at/doing business with a particular company. *See also* **brand.**

mass e-mail 1. an **e-mail** message sent to a large group, often the entire company **2.** any **e-mail** from someone you don't know that you delete without reading; frequent senders include the **CEO, HR,** and **corporate communications**. The reflex to delete mass e-mails may result in consequences like missing the renewal deadline for your **benefits. 3.** the completely impersonal and generic way heartfelt messages such as holiday greetings or expressions of sadness following a tragedy are communicated, providing little cheer or comfort **4.** how you are informed that the company is **merging** with another and that you're going to lose your job

massage 1. *n.* a therapeutic kneading of muscles administered to ease tension and relieve stress **2.** a pricey and fleeting relaxation tool, the need for which, due to stress, is directly proportional to the rate of pay increases received, causing one's monthly disposable net income to remain constant over many years despite advancement and promotions **3.** a bribe offered to employees in an attempt to lure them to a function or forum where information is dispensed and generate impressive attendance numbers (e.g., a "Health and Wellness" or "Work/Life" event); even though the massages last only ten minutes and are delivered in those chairs that make people look really stupid, many employees will show up just to get a massage in the middle of the workday, but still leave the event not having the foggiest idea of what it was promoting, although they will take a free pen or magnet with a **logo** on it because it's free. *See also* **premium.**

massage 1. *v.* to manipulate **2.** a kind of sensual way of saying "make it say what we want it to say," especially in regard to irrefutable factual data like research, **sales,** or performance statistics, i.e., lie, but not exactly lie **3.** what your **boss** says when he wants you to **change** something you did, but can't really figure out or verbalize exactly what he wants, e.g., "I'm thinking it would be better if you could massage this a bit to be more **customer-centric."**

May I ask who's calling? 1. an inquiry made by a secretary or **administrative assistant** to determine the identity of a caller **2.** "They're here, but let me see if you're important enough for them to talk to you"; close cousin of "Let me see if they're here"

meeting 1. a gathering called to discuss whatever "pressing" business is at hand. The bane of most corporate citizens' existence, hallmarked by wild inefficiency. Status meetings, scheduled on a regular basis (weekly, monthly), are prime opportunities to see your coworkers fight off sleep. Meetings may involve an agenda, listing **action items,** but this is in only the most organized, and possibly boring, marathon affairs. A petri dish for **office politics,** meetings are excellent forums for observing the subtle humiliation of various staff members and management intimidation techniques. Expect other staffers to say what you have expressed only minutes earlier and have the assembled group react with great enthusiasm, as if they have never heard this sentiment before. While many aspects of the meeting are unpredictable, you can rest assured than anything discussed will promptly evaporate into the ether within seconds of the gathering's adjournment, thereby necessitating another meeting in the future. When e-mailing a **colleague** about a relatively simple matter, you may be met with the response, "We should have a meeting about this." *Please note:* You may need to attend meetings to talk about the idea of having a meeting. *See also* **premeet.**

memo 1. *abbr* memorandum; a document created to convey business-related information **2.** with the advent of **e-mail,** a dinosaur, as the memo is confined to the realm of "hard copy," i.e., paper. As most information is now conveyed through **e-mail,** content that would have been previously communicated through a memo is reduced in importance by approximately 5,000 percent, as nobody really pays attention to/reads **e-mails. 3.** for some reason, some departments continue to actually produce memos, which only seems to underscore the irrelevance of the information they relay; typical generators of memos include **human resources,** the **cafeteria,** and facilities management. **4.** if for some reason any department in your company is still producing memos, you should to enlist the "time travel machine" known as the classifieds immediately and join the rest of us in the twenty-first century; you might also want to make a

donation to some antideforestation nonprofit for karma points while you're at it.

mental health day 1. a day taken off by employees who call in sick when they are not physically ill, but who require a day away from the office to effectively manage the stress of their job **2.** should be embraced and formalized as company policy everywhere, as everyone knows people take them, and the cerebral flush they provide no doubt actually does increase productivity and decrease the likelihood of employees going postal **3.** source of transparent, absurd, and much belabored theater of the "sick call," which includes early-morning phone messages delivered in anemic voices and punctuated by coughing or grave references to some bad sushi, a picnic potato salad, etc., and the unpleasant—and projectile—bodily functions they can inspire. *Please note:* Particularly evil bosses will call you at home to **bust** you while you're out at the movies. *See also* **sick day.**

mentor 1. a trusted counselor or adviser, typically older or more senior in rank to the person to whom they are providing guidance **2.** a benevolent, wise, and trustworthy member of an organization who provides advice and support to a junior employee in an effort to help that person develop professionally—on Earth Two **3.** a wonderful myth that is unfortunately not possible due to the fact that nobody will take the time to learn a junior staffer's name let alone provide her with professional advice and input—especially when the senior **managers** are much too busy expending their energy trying to keep young bucks from nipping at their heels **4.** gurus and guest speakers will attribute much of their mind-blowing, overall awesomeness to their mentors—of which they have had seven throughout their career (and in fact *still have:* in the form of "the eighty-year-old retired CEO of the printing plant in Texas where I worked on the warehouse floor when I was nineteen," or "the recent college grad who keeps me in touch with what all the kids are doing"). Meanwhile, you've yet to have one mentor. **5.** as part of **enterprise**-wide **initiatives**, companies may set up formal mentoring programs in which only the employees you would never want to mentor you participate, and an interest in a career in business development leads to a pairing with a middle **manager**

in accounting: "He works with numbers! Go **pick his brain!** And remember: You only get out of this what you put into it!" Senior employees paired with Generation X staffers will find that their mentees have no interest in actually learning anything from them and just want to know how their mentor can help them get a better job.

merger 1. the joining of two companies **2.** the joining of two companies, usually with the goal of **leveraging synergy** of the resulting company's resources **3.** there's a lot involved in this, but the upshot is you're going to lose your job unless you can finagle a choice spot on the merger **committee. 4.** source of major freakout mode amongst employees **5.** if two companies merge, the newly formed corporate entity will retain the name of the organization with the **brand** that is more **prestigious** or less marred by scandal, and the other company will just kind of fade away. *See also* **severance package, packaged out, deploy.**

meritocracy 1. a system that advances or promotes those of the greatest ability or talent **2.** a naive and very cute concept that many people entering the workforce will believe in. Upon learning that in fact the opposite is true, they will become bitter and angry like their fellow qualified and intelligent coworkers. *See also* **go-getter** and **up is down, down is up.**

micromanage 1. to supervise a project or employee in an extremely controlling and interfering manner **2.** quite simply: Hell. On. Earth.; one of the most grievous and prevalent sins committed in the business world. A demoralizing scourge that employees must endure and supervisors are never punished for because senior management doesn't really care how employees are treated **3.** the source of infinite misery of perfectly qualified employees and explains why the mild-mannered guy in the department spits psychotic venom at the **holiday party** or **drinks** after work **4.** ironically, a red flag for a **manager** who is completely **incompetent** and inefficient, as they *are not managing* (i.e., **delegating**) and make it impossible for people to do the jobs they were hired to do because their managers must be involved in every part of every task and in the end, slow things down **5.** fueled by a dysfunctional work environment infused with fear, a lack of trust, and, often, the mental illness of a **manager** who has been rewarded for his abusive behavior in the form of promotions and raises instead of being mandated to seek counseling

microwave popcorn 1. prepackaged popcorn that is made by heating it in a microwave **2.** remember Bugs Bunny cartoons and the anthropomorphized smell that, at the end of its wafting ephemeral trail, had a hand that sought out people and drew them, finger up one nostril, toward something?: it's like that. If someone makes popcorn on your floor, you will know it, and it will drive you crazy with desire, because you know it is indicative of that very rare species of snack that is both delicious and hot; you probably won't get any.

mindshare 1. consumer awareness of, and attentiveness to, a product or **brand 2. marketing** speak for brainwashing; calculated mind control achieved through tactics such as an enormous ad **budget, talent** endorsement, and mentions on the *Today* show or *Live! With Regis and Kelly.* Relies heavily on consumers believing that knowledge of something may indicate the quality of a product, and the fact that most people are sheep, incapable of critical or independent thought

miscommunication 1. an unclear communication **2.** what someone claims has happened when they have not communicated something at all and want to blame the addressee, e.g., "Oh, we must have had a miscommunication"; a classic **passive-aggressive** move **3.** what someone says when they are not getting what they want and they know the addressee is intentionally not giving it to them, e.g., "I think we're having a miscommunication"; sounds forgiving, but in this context carries the subtext "You idiot. Do it the way I want or I'm going to kick your ass." *See also* **disconnect.**

mission critical 1. essential to the ability to do business **2.** the application/program/database that when it fails or goes down completely disables a company or department, i.e., everyone takes a long lunch or goes home

mission statement 1. a summarization of an organization's goals and reason for being. **2.** A succinct, high-falutin' paragraph

that encapsulates the purpose of your company. Often includes the words service, creative, **innovative**, worldwide, opportunity, growth. Do not be surprised if when you read this, it resonates with you deeply, eerily reminding you of the company you work for—in opposite-land.

moderately qualified, nonthreatening white straight male employee who gets ahead because he's a "nice guy" (MQNWSMEWGABHANG) 1. a guy you work with **2.** infuriating to any very qualified female, minority, ethnic, or gay person he works with, as anything the MQNWSMEWGABHANG says is received with more respect, credibility, and veracity than anything his coworkers say, especially because he may be repeating verbatim what his more **invisible colleagues** have said to him, or senior management in another context or even in the same **meeting 3.** even more infuriating because **a:** he is not even aware of the fact that he is the recipient of special privilege, or **b:** he is

monetize 1. to translate consumer interface with a Web site into revenue **2.** to figure out, after you've programmed, designed, and marketed a really cool and **robust** Web site, how you're actually going to pay the electric bill; key to keeping one's job at an **Internet** company **3.** may result in absurd suggestions being pitched in the vacuum of a boardroom, that seem like something people might actually go for but when executed in real life elicit the consumer response of, "You want me to pay for that? Are you serious?"

morale 1. the spirit of a group **2.** in most organizations/departments, critically low, a fact that is painfully obvious to the people who work there and, amazingly, completely lost on or just ignored by management **3.** one of the first things to plummet in an organization led by poor management, but due to its amorphous nature—unlike **sales** figures, cogs produced, media mentions—hard to quantify, making the **goal** of good morale a priority of the lowest order; inability to measure morale ensures **incompetent,** abusive, negligent **managers** almost indefinite tenures, especially if they produce results—even if it's at the cost of all else. **Bottom line** message to employees: "The truth is, **we** really don't care how you feel."

move forward 1. to proceed or make progress **2.** another completely unnecessary way of saying something really simple; see preceding definition **3.** can also be used in a more aggressive spirit, i.e., to bulldoze, or continue to push something through regardless of the thoughts of the people a person is addressing. *Note:* not to be confused with **going forward.**

move from within 1. for an employee of a company to attain a more desirable position within that organization **2.** something your parents earnestly believe is possible—and will suggest to you when you call them on the phone **crying**—this is, in fact, extraordinarily difficult to accomplish, particularly if it means moving from one not so sexy department to another department perceived to be more fabulous, because once you do what you do, you are what you do, even if you studied **marketing**/fashion/English/film **3.** a myth perpetuated by true but rare success stories of people working their way up from the **mail room** in the Hollywood system or corporate America fifty years ago, which doesn't really apply anywhere else or exist anymore. *See also* **pigeonholed.**

move the needle 1. to exceed expectations on a project; often used in **sales 2.** an achievement that is often a **goal,** but rarely a reality, ensuring that it will never be on an employee's list of **KPI,** because then they might have to actually do it in order to get their **bonus**

multitasking 1. doing several things at once **2.** to work on many projects or tasks concurrently without compromising the results of any of them; essential workplace survival skill that usually turns out to be more like "multijobbing" because it often involves doing the work of more than one person **3.** a work style that, in **interviews,** many people will claim they are experts at, like it's some big accomplishment, when in reality it's kind of like saying "I'm not retarded"; many of those same employees will become overwhelmed and rendered useless should the number of responsibilities on their **plate** exceed three. **4.** participating in a **conference call** while balancing your checkbook and **e-mailing** a **friend;** IMing the **office flirt** while surfing the Web and filing your nails; sitting in a **meeting** while writing a grocery list and eating **lunch**

Myers-Briggs 1. a diagnostic test used to assess an individual's personality and behavioral preferences **2.** a diagnostic test that one may encounter in a workshop or **management training** seminar that involves answering a billion questions and ultimately brands you with a four-letter "type," i.e., INTJ or ENFP, which indicates if you Feel, Intuit, Sense, Judge, etc., that is supposed to enlighten you about how you deal with other people and the world **3.** if you've never done this, you feel that you will unlock the mysteries of your personality and why life sucks for you. That doesn't happen, but you will walk away thinking, "I'm an *intuitive* person. That's why my **boss** and **I** are having these **disconnects.**" You will also gain an immediate affinity for people who are classified similarly to you, feeling as if you are of the same "tribe" and that everyone else is an asshole.

N

nastygram **1.** an **e-mail** written in a punitive tone and sent with the **goal** of correcting and intimidating the recipient **2.** a petty and irritating bitch-slap, sent with the **goal** of defending the author's ridiculously small territory and authority and venting otherwise unexpressed frustration and anger; frequently sent from middle **managers** who must fight off the reality of their insignificance daily; a common tool of the **micromanager**

net-net **1.** the final result or outcome; the **bottom line 2.** an answer: it will work, or it won't work. Yes, or no. The forty-hour workweek would be abolished if people really used net-net on a regular basis. **3.** what someone says after they have bored you to tears with a three-hour **PowerPoint** presentation **4.** phrase that implies having actually done work in the form of **due diligence** or a deep dive; also very useful for cutting off irritatingly long-winded **colleagues** without saying, "Oh God, please shut up. What's the deal?" **5.** in a perversion of the phrase net-net, people may say the net-net is that you need to have another **meeting.**

network **1.** to pursue and create business contacts with the goal of fostering relationships both within and outside of your industry **2.** to just "work it," with the hope that someone you meet will hook you up with a job someday; occurs at **trade conventions, drinks** after work, **lunches, informational interviews,** etc. **3.** employees who network can be identified by their ability to seem fascinated by anyone who has a better job than they do, an aura that is irritatingly and apparently false to anyone who doesn't, and by the inch-thick wad of business **cards** they carry at all times and foist on their prey **4.** those who network will get the job you want, the promotion you deserve, regardless of their qualifications; get used to it, or start doing it. *See also* **kissing ass.**

nicknames 1. informal appellations frequently used when referring to those with whom the speaker is familiar, or for whom they have affection **2.** in the real world, these are an indicator of a close relationship between the person being referred to and the person using the nickname; at the **office,** the person spoken of probably **hates** the person using it, and most often the sobriquet used is not the actual nickname of the person being referred to, but some random made-up name that may in fact be a subtle constant reminder of the subject's faults or of something embarrassing they did five years ago **3.** cheap and easy way of implying familiarity while obscuring the fact that the person invoking the nickname could call the individual they're referring to "dog doo" if they wanted to, because they conduct their **performance review** and pay their salary **4.** classic **passive-aggressive** tactic used to subtly humiliate the subject of the nickname, as assigning a nickname

appears to be a friendly act, but **a:** the person who receives it usually doesn't have a say in what it is, and **b:** it can be something in the spirit of "big hips" or "country boy," which in general is not very well received by the person it is assigned to **5.** extremely lazy practitioners of the nickname will just shorten people's actual names like they're their freakin' best **friends,** which results in people calling others really stupid, almost unintelligible things like "Sha" (Sharon), "Gee" (Gina), and "Ka" (Katherine)—for some reason nobody seems to refer to men by truncated versions of their names. Weird, huh?

nimble 1. quick and agile **2.** frequently dropped word when discussing **goals,** usually used to describe an organization's or a person's ability to respond to rapidly **changing** circumstances **3.** absolutely impossible to be in the workplace due to a suffocating amount of red tape, rampant **micromanagement,** and the need for twelve people to sign off on the purchase of a ten-pack of Bic pens, which not only makes a company less nimble but paralyzes any task undertaken **4.** employees who show **initiative** and are **proactive**

with the **goal** of being nimble will inevitably be reprimanded with a **nastygram** from a **micromanager.**

nine to five 1. the hours of the workday **2.** so not the hours of the workday, but the only hours you are paid for **3.** really good movie made in 1980, with Dolly Parton making a surprisingly impressive turn as a secretary, Jane Fonda in big-ass glasses, and Lily Tomlin, who dresses up like Snow White; catchy title track. Features scenes of **boss** torture. Rent it.

no idea is a bad idea 1. phrase invoked in forums such as **brainstorming** sessions, problem-solving **meetings**, and workshops indicating a nonjudgmental atmosphere, with the **goal** of generating previously undiscovered or unspoken suggestions and thoughts **2.** a complete and total lie **3.** corporate cliché, usually disproved by the first ten seconds of any discussion following its declaration during which *someone has a bad idea,* which is met with blank stares, sympathetic nods, and the facilitator of the **meeting** saying "great" and writing it down **4.** pathetically easy bait—almost cruel, really— for younger members of the workforce and/or **interns** who actually believe it and have not yet learned what their more seasoned fellow attendees know all too well. *See also* **thinking outside the box, brainstorming.**

nonhierarchical 1. an organizational structure devoid of levels of increasing authority, or one that does not enforce ones that are implied **2.** first of all: not possible, as someone is always working for someone; you may hear the people at the top of the pyramid describe their organization this way, but you will not hear the **assistants** who are told when they can go to the **bathroom** doing so **3.** second of all, not realistic, as someone has to be in charge and make decisions; fashionable among **dot-com** firms during the boom, and we see how well that worked out

notebook 1. a small book of blank pages **2.** a small book of blank pages that people carry around with them for the purpose of writing "notes" in it to make it seem like they're paying attention in **meetings;** notes usually consist of memos to oneself regarding non–work related matters, or "doodles" that tend to look the same throughout a person's career, so much so that they make the author want to throw up on themselves, given they are so uninspired and predictable, even in moments of spacing out. Should an employee attempt to jot down thoughts in her notebook, these thoughts will be completely incomprehensible when she refers to them two weeks later. **3.** a prop every eager beaver out there carries to display their undying **initiative** and aid their vigilant **attention to detail;** these people actually do take notes, even in **meetings** about ordering from the **office supply catalog** and **fire drills 4.** a common company **premium** that advertises some corporate **initiative**

notice, to give 1. the act of informing your **manager** that you will be leaving your position within a specific amount of time **2.** source of many, many employee revenge fantasies, not because violence or retribution is involved, but just because the idea of walking into the **boss's** office and telling him you are leaving (AKA "You have no power over me anymore—jerk") is a scenario rivaled only by nir-

vana or a suspended state of carnal ecstasy, it frequently just doesn't seem attainable **3.** opportunity to say a final "You suck" to your **boss,** in the form of giving less than the standard two weeks' notice, which one can only hope temporarily cripples the department slightly and gives a faint glimmer of your value **4.** the period of time your **boss** has instructed you to give prior to taking a day off, a vacation, etc., that is never enough and, oddly, always changing, i.e., if he says he wants a month's notice for a day off, when you provide that, he will say he has received the request with too little notice, etc.; expect to see this infraction on your **performance review.** *See also* **once.**

NSFW 1. *lit* not safe for work **2.** essentially, something that a **blog** or other rogue Internet site points you toward, that for a variety of reasons (the most common is that it is slightly pornographic in nature) is the type of material that, if you're caught looking at, might get you fired; a way of the people looking out for the people. *Also see* **Internet usage policy.**

O

....

off the record 1. not for publication; spoken in confidence or unofficially **2.** "I'm not supposed to tell you this, and if you ever say I said it, I will categorically deny it. The fact that I am saying this is off the record absolves me of all responsibility for sharing this privileged information with you." **3.** also code for "Here comes some really good **gossip** about who is sleeping with whom," etc., and preface to information that will be the subject of **watercooler games** in the near future. *See also* **confidential.**

office 1. a room in which an employee conducts official business five days a week **2.** object of fierce and petty **office politics,** such as who gets one, who gets one with a window, who gets one in a corner, who is moved out of a **cube** into one, who has to share one, etc. **3.** possible saving grace, as it provides employees with some de-

gree of insulation from coworkers and the ability to shut the door to do work on a **résumé,** conduct a job **interview** over the phone, or have a nervous breakdown **4.** a place where people engaged in an **office romance** have sex

office flirt 1. staffer who engages in playful and innocuous amorous behavior that is understood to have no serious intentions **2.** male specimens, typically very attractive and charming, who tend to be more shameless in their behavior than their female counterparts, as the latter must be sensitive to crossing the line and being labeled the **office slut;** extraordinarily flattering to its subjects/marks, often to the point of boldness, causing many coworkers to develop crushes on them, or worse, to believe that a relationship is a possibility. Very adept at concealing whorish nature, which serves to further delude subjects that are his or her singular focus. Tend to be very effective in the workplace, as the constellation of people throughout the company crushing out on them will give them whatever they want, be it a file, a phone number, space on someone's calendar, etc. **3.** with few exceptions, these people are not available; at best, they are dating the person in the **office** next to you/a VP, at worst they have a live-in partner or wife and child. If confronted in any way about their behavior, will respond with a somewhat shocked/incredulous demeanor, saying "I have a girlfriend/boyfriend/wife," etc., underscoring a particularly pernicious aspect of their conduct, which is to prey on the desperate hopes of single people in the office and make them feel like pathetic losers, all in the service of bolstering their own ego **4.** unfortunately, even though they are evil, office flirts can often be the only reason you get up in the morning, add an element of intrigue and excitement to an otherwise boring setting, and they do make the time fly when lavishing their attentions.

office politics 1. the effect that interpersonal relationships have on business dealings between people and the work they are engaged in **2.** the foundation of all business transactions and decisions, from who sits next to the **boss** at the weekly **staff meeting** to who makes more money, who gets a **meeting,** who gets promoted, who gets the best **office** (*especially* who gets the best **office**), etc. Also, having the ability to befriend and gain the trust of those you are betraying/stabbing in the back (or being sharp enough to know who you can afford to screw over with minimal repercussions) is the key component of mastering office politics. If you want to get to the top of the heap, you're going to have to master office politics; possessing the ability to laugh riotously and readily at exec jokes that are not even remotely funny is a really good start. **3.** the reason why those who **kiss ass, manage up,** play **golf,** have **smooth hair,** and laugh a lot do so well in corporate America

office romance 1. an intimate relationship between coworkers at the same company **2.** an inevitable product of people spending more time with each other than they do with their friends or family **3.** really, really exciting and fun when blooming or just beginning, as they frequently require secrecy and therefore produce all kinds of tit-illating James Bond/cloak-and-dagger maneuvers (acting like you're **friends**/acquaintances in **meetings** or at company functions; booking two hotel rooms on a **business trip** but really using one; leaving the **office** at different times and meeting up at a predetermined location; spending the entire day **e-mailing** a paramour while pretending to do work; making up absurd and totally unconvincing excuses when coworkers run into you on the street together at 11:00 A.M. on a Sunday; and, of course, the after-hours screw on a desk; etc., etc., etc.). The joke, of course, is that employees pay much more **attention to detail** when it comes to figuring out who is sleeping with whom, and everybody knows about the affair, reducing a couple's "covert" shenanigans to pure comedy. **4.** due to an office romance's intoxicating nature, many employees involved in one will behave as if the affair will never end or that the fallout won't be that bad if it does. However, most crash and burn after the thrill is gone and the participants realize that the attraction was more circumstantial/libido-driven, at which point this situation becomes really, really uncomfortable and an obviously really bad idea. Af-termath may include having a public **crying** jag of mysterious origin; having to work every day with someone you rejected/someone who rejected you/someone who knows what you look like naked; nasty work-related retribution from a co-worker or superior who was previously helping your career; the **cold shoulder**, etc. **5.** the supervisor/**direct report** liaison is a particularly vile form of the phenomenon, given that the junior employee reaps the benefits of getting horizontal with the **boss,** no matter how "objective" the senior person claims to be, because it's kind of hard to be objective when someone is performing oral sex on you; also pathetically delusional, as those involved will firmly attest to their equitable nature despite the fact that one person clearly holds more power over the other

office slut 1. sexually promiscuous woman at the workplace **2.** yes, unfortunately, due to a gender-based cultural bias, this is pretty much always a woman; her guy counterpart is the **office flirt,** whom all the other dudes **hate**/admire/envy because he beds all the hot chicks **3.** the chick who sleeps with everyone, sometimes through serial dating, other times through post-**drinks** or **holiday party** hook-ups. Either way, no one can seem to understand why she insists on only dipping into the office pool to find partners in intimacy, like there's not a whole world out there for her to interface with. Coworkers also have difficulty comprehending why a person would want to create a situation in which the likelihood of being in a room where *multiple* people know what they look like naked is greatly increased.

office supplies 1. tools used to execute work-related tasks such as paper, pens, staplers, tape, etc. **2.** items small enough for you to steal and use at home, that the company doesn't keep close tabs on because of their lower cost relative to other operating expenses (unless of course, you're stealing in bulk, in which case you're just stupid and will get caught). Some employees may steal office supplies they don't even need because they feel like they're owed something, or need a relatively low-risk way to express their anger at the company or their **boss. 3.** object of corporate prisoner porn and cost-free shopping sprees via the office supply catalog, which in addition to selling envelopes, paper clips,

and scissors sells some really fun and cool shit, like nice pens with really smooth action, multicolored cubes of Post-it notes, jewel-toned folders and stamps that say CONFIDENTIAL and URGENT, not to mention entire **office** furniture sets, **microwave popcorn,** and industrial-size garbage cans. If you order office supplies, the day they arrive will be really exciting and kind of like Christmas/Hanukkah/Kwanzaa (see **diversity**). **4.** should too much theft of office supplies occur, you'll know it, as a lock will appear on the office supply cabinet or closet or the office supply catalog will need to be signed out from an **administrative assistant.**

offline, to have a conversation 1. confidentially; in a less formal context **2.** in an environment or under circumstances that will allow a person to honestly assess and elucidate a situation, i.e., give the real dirt on what's happening, possibly trash/rat out coworkers, reveal that someone is getting fired, someone **hates** someone else, someone had sex with someone, etc., all of which will be vehemently denied if ever brought up in the future **3.** to have a conversation at a later date or in another setting, because talking about it in a **meeting** will bore the hell out of fellow attendees **4.** to have a conversation away from a group of "witnesses" because you want to take someone's idea

off-site 1. a gathering off-site geared toward **team**-building and increasing productivity, often led by a **consultant** and featuring guest speakers. May involve exercises in which you identify your communication style, the **Myers-Briggs** test, catching the weird **accounts payable** guy in a "trust fall" exercise, and finding out that your coworker gardens or collects Fabergé eggs. May also involve heavy **drinking,** spiteful **gossip**, and making out with a guy from the **help desk**

old person 1. an individual who is advanced in years **2.** first of all, "old" is completely relative to the average age of employees within an organization, so you might find yourself old at fifty-five, but you might also find yourself old at forty. **3.** the staffer who is physically and intellectually more mature than the rest of the workforce at a company; could very well be around to serve as an ever-ready source of **institutional knowledge** ("Wait, when

did we do that?" "What was that division called?" "What did the press say about that ugly merge-purge situation?"); a product of a rare show of compassion by a senior exec, or because the company is afraid of an ageism lawsuit, even though these staffers are frequently confused by Outlook Express and are known to refer to the "Interweb"

on board 1. in agreement or supportive of **2.** agreeable to an idea that is unethical or illegal, or willing to ignore/not tell anyone about it

on point 1. extremely attentive and on top of things **2.** used in the context of a request from the **boss**, i.e., "Make sure you're on point with this project," which really means, "Make sure you don't screw this up, and the fact that I have to tell you this means you've screwed up before and I don't trust you."

on the same page 1. to be in agreement; to have a mutual and compatible understanding regarding an issue **2.** to agree! To have a mutual and compatible understanding regarding an issue! Why is that so hard to say? (PS: no one reads anymore, so very few people would be on a page, anyway.) **3.** "we are all going along with this, even if we think it's based on faulty logic, ridiculous, disingenuous in its claims, etc."

on time 1. to arrive at a place in the **time frame** previously agreed upon between two parties **2.** 9:00 A.M., 9:30, whatever it's supposed to be. Whatever **3.** something **managers** are sticklers about, if only because it is a thing they can empirically measure, understand, and, most important, hold against you if you are late to work **4.** unless you're coming in at 11:00 A.M., a meaningless standard that has no effect on the quality of your work; those who come in at nine on the dot can be grossly **incompetent** and lazy, but if they're there on time, they dodge the bullet that nails their occasionally late but efficient, smart, and more hardworking **colleagues. 5.** inefficient and laughably condescending **check-ins** will occur regarding an employee's tenminute delay in reporting to work; one would think that someone who gets paid a lot more than you would have more important things to do than reprimand you for not reporting for duty at the appropriate hour, but apparently with the title of **man-**

ager comes the responsibilities of being a babysitter. **6.** employees who have **bosses** obsessed with their staff being on time will be met with frustrating and unavoidable real-life circumstances that impede their **commute** and be overwhelmed with panic when they cannot make a call to inform their supervisor (or the supervisor's assistant) of a delay due to a bad cell phone connection, being trapped in the subway where there is no cell phone reception, or because of a nonfunctioning pay phone.

once 1. to occur a single time **2.** to occur all the time, i.e., if you are not **on time** once, you will be considered late all the time; if you forget to print out a status report once, you will be considered unreliable; if you neglect to deliver a phone message once, you will lack **attention to detail**. Backbone of **performance reviews**; you won't get a raise or promotion because you did something once, indicating that you are not ready to be advanced to the next level, are not "management" material yet, etc.

110 percent 1. *idiom* more than is expected, to exceed expectations **2.** whatever. An annoying— and you know, *technically* *impossible*—way of describing one's performance, or in most cases, effort. Which if you think about it, doesn't mean jack, because you can *give* 110 percent (hell, you can give 112 percent!) and still not produce 82 percent, which is like a low B. **3.** much easier to say than exerting the mental effort to describe how one actually goes to great lengths to achieve **goals,** which is a big part of why this is overused. *See also* **perfection, excellence.**

one-off 1. a job or activity that is done only once **2.** vaguely obscene-sounding term that is unnecesarily used when asking, "Is this the only time we're going to do this?"

onetime expense 1. a cost that is incurred a single time **2.** a way of justifying and writing off a costly, and huge, mistake **3.** the extraordinarily expensive cost of remodeling the new SVP's **office** and floor

open architecture 1. an environment that encourages creative thinking **2.** very elegant and fancy way of saying, "We want to encourage people to be **innovative,**" which is proved false when anyone tries to suggest new or creative ways of do-

ing things; if a very good idea is produced by a staffer, management will seize upon it and take credit for it, significantly reducing the employee's sense of **ownership** and his willingness to be a **team player,** not to mention the likelihood of another very good idea ever being suggested. *See also* **thinking outside the box.**

open door policy 1. the idea put forth by employees in a managerial or supervisory position that junior staffers should feel free to approach them with any concern, question, or issue in the workplace **2.** completely meaningless and untrue 98 percent of the time; a phrase invoked by all **managers** either instinctively or because they heard it in a company-sponsored **management training** workshop; distant cousin of "there are no stupid questions" and **"no idea is a bad idea" 3. managers** who stress their open door policy will always be the ones who are most intimidating and will greet you with an icy stare should you approach the threshold of their **office. 4.** code for, "If you want to rat out one of your coworkers, please feel free to do so at any time." **5.** An employee who attempts to take advantage of an open door policy will encounter a variety of responses, including sympathy followed by inaction and/or amnesia; an interruption in the form of an urgent phone call or **meeting** the **manager** must attend to immediately, with the promise of **circling back** to the issue at a later date; or the phrase, "You need to be part of the solution, not part of the problem."

open lines of communication 1. an environment among members of a group that allows and encourages the exchange of information **2.** something a lot of people are *really into,* who will remind you that they want this and strive for it all the time, to the point that invoking this idea becomes a kind of Pavlovian response that kicks in at the end of every conversation or interaction. Of course, many people really stress having open lines of communication, except regarding all of the stuff they'd never tell you in a million years, and all the stuff they really don't want to hear about from you.

opportunity 1. a circumstance that is advantageous **2.** a word used when talking to superiors about a screwup or unfortunate situation in order to put a posi-

tive spin on it, e.g., "Missing this **deadline** really presents us with the opportunity to see how the **team** operates under a tighter **time frame,**" or "The fact that we have no **marketing budget** gives us an opportunity to **challenge** the **team** to **think outside the box** and test the effectiveness of our **viral marketing** strategy." *See also* **growth opportunity.**

org chart 1. *lit* organizational chart; a schematic representation of the reporting structure of an institution **2.** a symbolic diagram illustrating where people are on the food chain; really hits home when you see yourself at the bottom; source of the phrase **dotted line,** as in management

organic 1. to be the result of a natural and uncalculated process **2.** word used to describe a process you don't know how to explain, or to help you avoid being pinned down by specifics, because what you're talking about isn't calculated or sanitized and can't be quantified so definitively, dude **3.** a word used to position anything while imbuing it with a certain mystery and unpredictability that, even so, will, due to its organic origins, lead to trustworthy results **4.** smoke screen for "I don't have a plan. I'm just winging it."

out-of-office reply 1. an automated **e-mail** message sent to notify people that the respondent is not at work **2.** the last thing you do before leaving for vacation or a business trip; is extraordinarily liberating and makes you feel like you have just become **invisible;** an awesome digital brick wall that no one can argue with **3.** the totally best version of this is the "as of X date, 200X, I am no longer working at X place, full of losers. Please use redhot mamma7984@hotmail.com if you need to contact me. **Thanks**"; even if you've been laid off, it's still awesome because you know you don't have to answer any of those people who wrote you all the time *ever again.*

outgrow your position 1. to expand in skill and experience beyond your current job **2.** what you are told you have done after delivering above and beyond and 110 **percent,** attending **management training** sessions, **pushing the envelope**, and being a **superstar**, because what you've really done is outperform your **boss** and become a threat; your re-

ward is that there's no room for growth or money in the **budget** to accommodate your **excellence.**

outing 1. a non–business related group excursion organized with the goal of having fun, **team building,** and improving **morale 2.** even though it's on the company dime and may involve free food/entertainment/getting out of work a couple of hours early, it's still mandated "fun," which, of course, is no fun at all, especially when it's with people you see all day, some of whom you can't stand; examples include laser tag, bowling, picnics, museum outings, sporting events, etc.; will inevitably result in coworkers inquiring surreptitiously to their most trusted **colleagues** what the earliest professionally acceptable and least punitive time to leave is while they all act like this is the greatest time they've ever had **3. managers** who organize these activities think they are the greatest supervisors ever, and that the little people love outings and don't realize that it is a complete waste of company funds, as most people would really rather just work until 5:30, go home and catch a *Law & Order* on cable, and then go out for **drinks** with their real coworker **friends** when they feel like it, as opposed to being mandated to socialize.

ownership 1. to be invested in work and take responsibility for it, due to a genuine feeling of having made a meaningful contribution with it **2.** something management insists they want everyone to "have a sense" of regarding their work while simultaneously breaking down tasks into increments so small that a feeling of contributing to something larger or meaningful is next to impossible

P

packaged out 1. when a staffer's job is redefined through a restructuring process that results in the de facto termination of their employment and the awarding of a **severance package 2.** a very convenient, uncontroversial, and tidy way for **managers** to get rid of employees they don't like; **incompetent** employees will also be packaged out, in accordance with the corporate axiom that those who can't do their jobs will be rewarded for their shortcomings.

pain points 1. weaknesses in an organization 2. euphemism for where things are really screwed up; sounds like a minor crick in your neck after a bad night's sleep or muscle soreness after a slightly strenuous workout, but really describes the places where the company is rotting from the inside out, where nothing can get done due to crippling inefficiency and/or suffocating bu-

reaucracy and unchecked **incompetence 3.** a phrase frequently employed by **consultants** when addressing executives as a way to softball bad news and avoid hurting their feelings; key to **consultant** keeping the lucrative contract with the corporate **client**

panic button 1. a location on a Web site that contains a link to another, usually less controversial site 2. escape hatch that those who surf **NSFW** Web sites [*read:* ones that contain nudity] on the job use to avoid being **busted**

paradigm 1. a universally accepted idea or way of thinking 2. what everybody believes, the way things are done because they've been done like this forever 3. used to mystify and intimidate **colleagues**/customers/ **clients** who are ideally short-circuited by the use of such a fancy word, especially one that contains a silent "g"; far too sophisticated and intellectual a word to be bandied about in the workplace, especially because the majority of people who use it have no idea what it means. Those who have **drunk the Kool-Aid** will speak of a "dominant paradigm" (which is kind of redundant, no?) and **paradigm shifts.**

paradigm shift 1. when change causes a widely believed way of thinking to need adjustment, or to become outdated and be discarded altogether **2.** everything discussed above regarding **paradigm,** with the added sexiness/ diceyness of discussing **change,** which scares the hell out of people **3.** organizations weighed down by old-school thinking and execs will talk about this all the time, because they realize that if they don't learn new tricks fast, they're toast. *Also see* **change.**

parking lot 1. a metaphorical space onto which issues not included on an agenda are tabled for consideration at a later date; may be physically represented by a **whiteboard** or other such device **2.** where the issues that **a:** nobody wants to talk about, **b:** are too controversial, **c:** re-

quire too much work, or **d:** are irrelevant points that someone with their own agenda tries to slip into the conversation, are shelved; of course, none of these matters are ever addressed and will therefore repeatedly surface on **meeting** agendas as **action items**, and meet the same fate.

pass the buck 1. to defer responsibility to another party **2.** common survival tactic used to avoid catching heat for anything; similar to a child's game of musical chairs or "hot potato"—if in the end you got it, you're gonna get it **3.** senior management, when challenged by their **boss,** will instantly pass buck to their anonymous **team,** and then institute Draconian policies to rectify "problems" in their department, where they have no clue of how things actually work or get done; spineless coworkers will pass the buck with abandon, then wonder why you don't want to have **lunch** with them, but they'll still get promoted and become your **boss. 4.** passing the buck can result in furious **e-mail** forwarding, involving an infinite amount of respondents attempting to locate the source of the **blame** for a situation.

passion 1. intense and overwhelming enthusiasm or emotion **2.** a feeling that **managers** will demand of their employees while giving them no reason to have any; supervisors who harp on a **team's** lack of passion will consistently thwart factors that could possibly encourage the development of some form of passion, such as autonomy or recognition for a job well done **3.** big with the **consultants,** who say, ad nauseam—in presentations, on their Web sites, etc.—that they bring passion to everything they do, and that this is the largest contributing factor to their success; will often invoke the term when discussing the management of the "industry of me"

passive-aggressive 1. to express negative feelings through nondirect and unassertive behavior **2.** extremely common behavior in the workplace and executed by employees at all levels in an organization. Examples include: your **boss** telling you it's okay to leave at 5:30, but repeatedly calling you at 5:50 to show they know you're not there; a **boss** expecting you to stay at the **office** until they leave, and then staying at work until seven making personal phone calls within earshot of you; a habitually late employee who has been spoken to about the importance of being **on time** and who repeatedly vows to change his ways, and then comes in late every day anyway; a fellow employee asking someone, "Does my Outlook not connect to your Outlook? Should I call the **help desk** to sort this out?" when they're just pointing out that you didn't respond to their message; someone constantly rescheduling a **meeting** on a topic they don't want to discuss, or not inviting someone to a **meeting** they should attend as a tactic to shut them out

peel the onion 1. to get to the heart or root of a matter **2.** to solve one problem only to find another problem that has to be fixed, and upon solving that one, discovering a few more, ad infinitum **3.** in the context of **sales** calls, or **client** or pitch meetings, the act of slowly stripping away layers of an **issue** in an intriguing and engaging manner that ultimately wins over the audience—not really possible unless Garrison Keillor has suddenly joined your **team**

per 1. according to [per your request, instructions, etc.] **2.** no one knows what this really means, but it sure sounds fancy/kind of legalese when you begin a memo with it or use it in the title of your **e-mail;** indicative of a **CYA** or **FYI e-mail** and possible mind-numbing content to follow

perception 1. what is observed and believed to be true, which may differ from reality **2.** The. Number. One. Name of the game. All that matters; you can be a total fuckup, but if people think you're doing a good job, you're fine. **3.** applicable in too many areas to mention, but among them: bad supervisors who expertly **manage up;** job candidates with Ivy League pedigrees who are less qualified than their less expensively educated competitors; completely insane/drug-dependent people who keep it together long enough in crucial situations to seem competent; the totally lazy/negligent staffer who affects a harried and stressed-out demeanor to give the impression of being overworked; the successful and/or prestigious company that everyone wants to work for, which is really a horrible place to work and views its overrated reputation as a substitute for paying competitive wages **4.** in one of the great injustices of the workplace, those who are badly perceived for anything—from less-than-fashionable wardrobe choices to regional affiliation—will be the first ones to be let go, rightsized, downsized, laid off, even if they're more conscientious or qualified than those who are perceived to be better than them but are actually less skilled. **5.** a corporate truth intimately understood by those well schooled in the art of **kissing ass**

perfection 1. a state of being free from error or without defect **2.** not unlike **excellence,** a word that is "perfectly" fine on its own, but when used as a benchmark or **goal** to measure **performance** in corporations that are dysfunctional, bloated, weighed down with red tape, and rife with **office politics,** is patently absurd **3.** a phrase used by guest speakers or gurus who swoop in, do their song and dance, and advocate demanding nothing less than "perfection"—after all, that's what they demand, and a job worth doing demands nothing less than **110 percent**, or perfection, doesn't it?—and then leave and take their check, perfectly **4.** a reprise of definition **1**: to be perfect is to be free from error.

That means no mistakes. So, therefore, people who say they accept nothing less than perfection/produce nothing less than perfection are blowing smoke *out* their ass, blowing smoke *up* your ass, and are essentially lying. If they spent as much time making sure they or the people who work for them did a "great" or even "good" job, they would be far ahead of the game, not to mention a lot more believable and trustworthy.

performance review 1. an annual formal evaluation of an employee's work **2.** the yearly ritual during which your **boss** sits you down and tells you all the things you screwed up over the last twelve months. In some cases you will have been given **feedback** on your mistakes at the moment they occurred, and repeatedly in the months following the mistake; however, this is another perfectly good opportunity for the **boss** to again remind you of your shortcomings, with the added bonus of documenting it for your permanent personnel file. The bad things you did **once** will be **called out** and identified as areas that present a **growth opportunity,** and you will be forced to invent (and act like you care about) **goals** for expanding your **skill set** in the coming year, which will probably be shaped by your **boss's** desire to pawn off more of his work on to you under the guise that he is going to be concentrating more on the **big picture. 3.** in other cases you will be under the impression that you have done a perfectly fine job all year, only to be completely blindsided by a list of complaints that you hear about for the first time during your review. **4.** in either case, you must sit there respectfully, hearing about how much you suck as your blood reaches a rolling boil; should you attempt to refute any of the charges against you, you will be told that you do not take **constructive criticism** well (a topic that is already addressed in your **goals**); in other words, you can't win. Your actual **goal** should be to get in and out of the boss's office as quickly as possible. **5.** at some companies, at the conclusion of your review, you will be asked to sign a statement verifying that this information has been discussed with you, which your **boss** will remind you is not an indication that you agree with it; although this is true, signing it still feels like you are, in fact, agreeing to the list of unsubstantiated lies enumerated in the document. Best of all, there may also be a space on the review where you can comment on, or disagree with, the information discussed, which your **boss** will also helpfully point out to you, as he cackles inside, knowing you'll never write anything in that space because they would just make your life more difficult if you did so. **6.** the final judgment on your performance will be measured by how well you "meet expectations" (i.e., you did not meet them, you met them, or you exceeded them), which is funny, because no one ever told you what their expectations were in the first place, other than that you should be **on time.**

perk 1. *slang:* perquisite; an advantage to working at a company that comes in the form of free or discounted goods and services **2.** in the formal sense, anything ranging from no-cost admission to a museum and cheap tickets to movies to 10 percent off the local Applebee's or a weekly case of beer (get drunk on us—really!) that makes it more desirable to work at a company; AKA no- / or low-cost bribe to placate The People while the execs enjoy favors and special treatment like courtside tickets to NBA games **3.** in the informal sense, the vaguely sexy intangibles that **managers** dole out as "favors" to their employees while acting like they're the benevolent giver of all things: tickets to a company event (procured at the last minute to emphasize the favor, which only means someone ahead of you turned them down); the "opportunity" to work a corporate function without pay where an attempt at **networking** will be met with a prompt bitch-slapping, or to attend a **benefit dinner**

permalancer 1. a freelance employee whose assignment is indefinite but whose hours and duties are precisely the same as their full-time staff counterparts **2.** people who endure all the same burdens, headaches, and demands that their salaried coworkers are subjected to, without any of the benefits the staffers receive, like . . . health **benefits**! Or paid time off or personal/**sick days,** or a **bonus.** Of course, even though these employees are expected to work the same long hours that staff employees do, they do not receive **overtime.** In short: all of the responsibility of a staffer with none of the advantages of working freelance **3.** a chief complaint in the perennially freelance community, which cripples **morale** and foments bad attitudes; management's response to such discontent will be **"if they don't like it, they can leave." 4.** a common cost-saving strategy in highly competitive or desirable industries such as fashion, entertainment, publishing, television production, etc., because employers can get away with it, as opposed to other professions, where the idea of taking or offering a job without benefits is considered lunacy, if not criminal

personal project 1. a task that is unrelated to company business **2.** one of the most insulting and demoralizing requests from executives, which involves dedicating time and work to a job that employees are not paid to do, but that exploits their abilities and talent, e.g., drafting the invite to a family reunion, coordinating the mass-mailing of save-the-date cards for the **boss's wedding,** creating a spreadsheet cataloging a superior's Pez dispenser collection, creating labels for the **CEO's** CD catalog, retouching a massive photo of an SVP's wife in a

bikini for her surprise fortieth birthday party—and then mounting it on a two-by-three-foot piece of foamcore **3.** each job of this nature will be prefaced by the statement "I have a really important project for you . . ." and the demand to be handled with the utmost priority, which means it trumps all the real work you had scheduled; after an employee has spent the entire day being **micromanaged** in his Web research of the area's best strip clubs, he will be reprimanded for not completing the actual work he had planned to do that day and be advised that he needs to work on his **time management** skills. **4.** anything you do on the clock under the **boss's** nose: freelance work, planning your **wedding,** writing your novel, completing assignments for your real estate license class, etc.

pick your brain 1. to informally get information or an opinion from someone **2.** to ask someone's opinion about something, take it, and act like it's your own **3.** ew, that's gross

pigeonholed 1. to be thought of as a person who does one thing to the extent that it is believed he cannot do anything else **2.**

you took a job because you needed a job, or because it was in an industry you wanted to break into, or because it sort of used your **skill set,** or maybe you even wanted it—but then you can never get out of the job because it becomes what you do, and are. Examples include: the proofreader who wants to be an editor, the tech support guy who wants to be a programmer, the salesperson who wants to be in **marketing,** the art assistant who wants to be a designer, the **trade publication** editor who wants to be a consumer magazine journalist, the **mail room** guy who wants to be a Hollywood agent. *See also* **move from within.**

pikers 1. potential **clients** who have a small amount of resources **2. sales** guy talk referencing pike fish; the people/ **clients** who are "small game" and kind of a waste of time and energy but have to be dealt with anyway; will receive less attention and bribes than more potentially lucrative prospects

pipeline 1. the reservoir of customers awaiting the delivery of a product or services **2.** a term very big among **sales** and **marketing** people, who will invari-

ably assert that the pipeline is "full" regardless of whether it's busting at the seams or dry as a bone **3.** demand may be inflated through the optimistic interpretation of what, exactly, it means to be a customer, i.e., those who seem very likely to contract business; those who **sales** staffers know have no intention of buying but whom they have just begun attempting to bribe with **dinners** and NFL tickets; those who **sales** has heard of

planful 1. you're kidding, right? *See also* **impactful** and **incentivize.**

plants 1. any of various photosynthetic, eukaryotic, multicellular organisms of the kingdom Plantae that characteristically produce embryos, contain chloroplasts, have cellulose cell walls, and lack the power of locomotion (um . . . got that?) **2.** completely harmless organic things that people put around their desk or **cube** in an attempt to improve their quality of life during the **nine to five 3.** living organisms, sometimes oddly banned from work spaces due to the fact that they are deemed **"unprofessional"** or "distracting," even though only the most twisted soul would take offense with a PLANT, which has no opinions and just sits there producing oxygen [*Tip to **cube** residents:* philodendrons don't need a lot of light and are really hard to kill.]

plate 1. matters to be dealt with **2.** what plate, nobody knows, but people always ask what's on it or say they have a lot or too much on it, when they really could be talking about what needs to be done **3.** claiming you have too much on your plate is a diplomatic way of saying you won't do something while also making you seem like a hard worker because your plate is so full already, and there's not even room for a side of mashed potatoes or the importing of data into an Excel sheet. *Also see* **bandwidth, push back.**

play in his/her sandbox, don't want to 1. to reject involvement **2.** invoked to avoid getting sucked into an ongoing feud, a rivalry, or inane politics between others: "Yo, that is some nasty shit and I'm not going there." **3.** blatant reference to cutthroat schoolyard politics of children that is refreshingly honest and appropriate

plays well 1. is enthusiastically received by; often used to de-scribe consumer reaction **2.** applicable in the context of a corporation or the marketplace, code for "X group reliably eats this up; consider them **low-hanging fruit**," e.g., "Clip art plays really well with senior management. I'd like to see more of it in this **deck. Thanks**"; "Glitter is playing really well with the tweens right now. The **client** doesn't have the **budget** for actual glitter, but I'd love to see a **logo** that perfectly mimics the look of glitter without actually using it. **Thanks in advance for your help.**"

please advise 1. request for input or information **2.** common **e-mail** parlance for "you go do all the work to get an answer to this question. No touch-backs." **3.** or, when written by a junior employee, indicates, "I've been asking you about this for days/weeks, and I can't do anything until you tell me what you want, so tell me already."

please shut the door 1. a request to shut the door to an **office** or **conference** room **2.** if you're asked this, you're about to get reamed, **fired,** fondled, or told that your entire department is being restructured in a way that will totally rock your world and have a direct impact on your day-to-day work life—surprise!

postmortem 1. a **meeting** held following the conclusion of a project to discuss its strengths and weaknesses **2.** billed as a constructive forum geared toward improving a **process,** but really a **meeting** in which everyone sits around trying to **blame** someone else for anything that went wrong; as a result of a postmortem, new unrealistic procedures that just make for more **administrative assistant** work and **FYI e-mails** will be instituted, but these will, more often than not, not come to pass. **3.** employees who hope to hold someone else accountable for a mistake that they always make will be bitterly disappointed by the postmortem, as any mistake, regardless of how many times it happens, will somehow be explained away as the result of a unique circumstance never before encountered and was therefore impossible to anticipate. **4.** by the time a postmortem rolls around, many people will have erased all memory of the project from their minds and be extremely aggravated that they have to take time away from their current project to attend the **meeting.** *Also see* **onetime expense.**

PowerPoint presentation 1. Microsoft (see **eight-hundred-pound gorilla**) application used to create slides integrating text and graphics for use in presentations **2.** low-tech, very ugly medium often stuffed with graphs, charts, plenty of jargon, and, in an effort to "mix things up" or make them more entertaining, generic clip art from the eighties and crazy colors; reduces even the most complex of issues to a few bullet points per page, thereby providing a formidable smoke screen for messy details—especially if they look pretty. *Also known as* **decks.**

PR people 1. public relations people; may also be known as publicists **2.** responsible for everything you see in magazines, on TV, in the newspaper, etc., and why a celebrity you haven't thought about for three years is suddenly everywhere you turn **3.** often very-well-put-together people who excel at talking to basically anyone at any time **4.** due to frequent work with/representing **talent,** have a high tolerance for egomaniacs, prima donnas, and other assorted temperamental folk

praise 1. an expression of approval or commendation **2.** M.I.A.; doesn't really happen

3. circumstances that may result in an appearance by the elusive praise: you're not getting a raise or promotion even though you do a great job (i.e., talk is cheap); a **manager** is known to negatively affect **morale** by being extremely critical and is being **coached** to address this **issue,** which will result in really awkward and pathetic exchanges featuring the **manager** "practicing" giving positive **feedback** to an employee; a **manager** is in a good mood because he or she is having an **office romance** and/or got laid.

premeet 1. a meeting that takes place before another **meeting,** with the purpose of preparing for it **2.** calendar-clogger that attempts to make sure everyone is **on the same page,** i.e., nobody is going to contradict anyone; we're not going to mention this; this is how we're going to spin this bad information; I will talk first and then you will go, etc. **3.** a gathering of politically aligned, like-minded people convened for the purpose of creating and discussing the strategy for a **meeting 4. a meeting** to set an agenda for a future **meeting; meeting** to talk about having a **meeting,** if you will. A time to discuss possible **action items** for a future **meeting.** A

huge waste of time. *See also* **follow-up.**

premium 1. a free gift given out at **trade conventions, conferences,** company fairs, corporate events, etc., for promotional use **2.** what most of us see and get: junk. A flimsy key chain (**thanks**—I need that!), a cheap pen, an ugly T-shirt you wear to the gym (or sleep in if it's too heinous for public consumption), a magnet emblazoned with a corporate slogan or **logo,** a cheap canvas bag (the best of them) **3.** despite their uselessness, many individuals are drawn to premiums like moths to a flame or hungry wolves to a rare rib roast and will in fact pocket half a dozen of them if they think they can get away with it; the reason—they are free. This is perhaps an indication of employees' unconscious feeling of a low-grade deprivation at all times, but it is more likely that people are just cheap and greedy. **4.** for the lazy/neglectful parent, a great gift for the **kids** when mommy or daddy return home from being away on business **5.** for people of "importance" (*read:* value) [ad sales, execs, celebs], a higher grade of premium exists in the form of high-style cocktail sets, fashionable watches, gift certificates to premier retailers, Swarovski-encrusted cell phones and iPods; these of course go to the people who can afford to buy any of these items and are also known in common vernacular as bribes. *See also* **gift bag.**

imosity and resentment between these two factions will often develop, with one being thought of as privileged, snobby, free-loading nancy boys and the other as tacky and crass plebeians with no taste.

prestige 1. a high level of respect and distinction **2.** companies will aggressively **leverage** any kind of prestige they have and go to great lengths to preserve it/perpetrate its myth in the marketplace, as it is an essential component of their **brand**. In many cases this reputation will be built on successes long since past or by founders with **vision** who are long since dead. **3.** in companies that produce a wide variety of products for multiple, and frequently different, audiences (such as magazine publishers, television and movie businesses, etc.), the **brands** of prestige will often be considered the crown jewels of the organization despite the fact that they never turn a profit. The less-prestigious **brands** (i.e., the ones that people actually buy and therefore make money) will be looked down upon, even though they pick up the slack of the more prestigious **brands** and in fact enable them to exist at all. Understandably, great an-

proactive 1. to initiate activity regarding an issue, particularly one that may present challenges **2.** to know what you are supposed to do before your **boss** tells you what he wants, when he has never indicated what he wants, except for the fact that he doesn't want you to do anything without **checking in** with him first **3.** what you are told you need to be more often when your **boss** has screwed up or been **busted,** i.e., "You need to be more on top of covering my ass, and it's your fault I made a mistake, because if you were more proactive, the mistake essentially would not have happened." *Also see* **initiative, nimble.**

process 1. a sequence of actions that leads to the accomplishment of a **goal 2.** a vague and mystifying way of saying "how something is done"; may come under fire from **consultants,** who will seek to remove any inefficiencies or **pain points,** which they will inevitably find, even if they have to make them up or pay someone else to suddenly create one

promoting from within/internal recruitment 1. hiring employees from within an organization and placing them in other, potentially more desirable or senior positions. **2.** a nice idea that the company is "deeply **committed** to" that doesn't seem to have documentation (i.e., Where are the people who have been hired from within? No one can find any). Internal job postings serve as a formidable smoke screen, creating the illusion of opportunity. *See also* **move from within.**

push back 1. to counter an idea; respectfully object **2.** a nice, **passive-aggressive** way of saying, "Are you out of your mind?" or "There's no way in hell that's happening." **3.** no

push the envelope 1. to exceed previously understood limits; innovate **2.** an overused phrase employed with the **goal** of directing and motivating employees to exceed expectations, without providing any of the tools, or money, to do so. *See also* **think outside the box.**

put a stake in the ground 1. to set limits with a **client,** customer, or coworker **2.** that is to say, "You asshole. We know your habit of taking advantage of and overworking our staff, asking for heaven on a plate for a budget of $2.53, and changing your mind at the last minute while still demanding a superior product on time and below cost. We're not going to take it. But we'll still deliver you a really nice cellophane **gift basket** full of chocolate, dried fruits, and nuts come holiday time. It's all good."

Q

....

quit 1. to leave, often abruptly **2.** like giving **notice,** the source of countless employee fantasies, but these reveries are more intense, extremely detailed, often dramatic, and, let's be honest, sometimes violent. Variants include the calm, cool, and collected walkout in midday, never to return; calling a **boss's** bluff and getting up and leaving in the middle of some **constructive feedback;** and the balls-to-the-wall, take-no-prisoners explosion during which the employee tells (*read:* yells) the **boss** how much they **hate** him, and, in fact, how much every one they work with hates him. May, in fact, even include the declaration "I QUIT!" because if you're gonna do it, you might as well do it in classic style **3.** an action that **benefits** keeps in check in most cases **4.** should you have a strong urge to quit, you might want to check with your therapist, because it might just be that your meds aren't working. *See* **antidepressant.**

R

....

radio silence 1. *idiom* the absence of correspondence, **feedback,** or information **2.** someone's not talking to/**e-mailing**/calling you; a highly suspect circumstance that may communicate extreme displeasure from higher-ups or the fact that you are about to be laid off. Whatever the reason, a cause for concern, unless it's just someone being **passive-aggressive** and ignoring your concern/request/question, which is entirely possible

ramp up 1. to increase activity, usually in preparation for something **2.** the period of time prior to a deadline when management realizes that everything is behind and they start to panic, resulting in emergency strategy **meetings,** an increased **sense of urgency,** and lots of overtime without pay **3.** a time of intense pressure during which some staffers will start to lose it/pick up the pack-a-day smoking

habit they kicked five years ago **4.** employees will be expected to sacrifice sleep, basic hygiene, and all quality of life while demonstrating singular dedication and enthusiasm to a project; those who do not will be told they have a bad attitude, are not a **team player,** and will continue to hear about this behavior in every one of their subsequent **performance reviews** for years to come **5.** the period of time preceding a **rollout**

reach out 1. to enlist the help of or involve in a process **2.** to pick up the phone, tell someone what you're doing, and ask if they will be part of it; often people will reach out to their **friends,** i.e., "I'm going to *reach out* to our *friends* in strategic partnerships to see if they'd like to come **on board** for this one." **3.** although this has a cooperative tone, those who are reached out to may in reality be

137

told they are going to become involved in a project whether they like it or not.

rebrand 1. to create a new identity for a company, often by changing its name, **logo,** or slogan, or some combination of the three **2.** a drastic measure undertaken in an attempt to distance a company from a sullied identity and trick consumers, or investors, who may have cooled on a **brand** due to scandal (WorldCom is now MCI), the distribution of a controversial product (Philip Morris is now the completely generic Altria), or the company's scary monolithic positioning (ADM, formerly "Supermarket to the World," is now pleasingly "Resourceful by Nature")

receptionist 1. employee who mans the front desk of a department/company and receives and fields incoming calls at the organization's main switchboard **2.** the meagerly paid person whose schedule is first and foremost dictated by the start and end of the business day and who witnesses all of the people who get paid more than them stroll in at 10:30; as a result, a deep bitterness may take root in their soul; may be required to man the phones at all times, which results in the humiliating act of effectively making other people aware of every time they go to the **bathroom** because they need to find someone to cover for them **3.** sees everything, and due to extreme periods of **boredom** is sensitive to ongoing workplace dramas and **office politics** and may revel in liberally spreading workplace **gossip;** may be discreet, but often is a mole for senior management, seeking a sense of importance and power by ratting out the people they welcome with a smile in the morning **4.** may also be the most generous and kind soul in a company, the one person you can count on to **CYA** and look out for you; will often know more about what's happening in the company than you do

recruiter 1. person hired by a company to seek out and screen qualified candidates for an open position within the organization **2. HR** working for commission; parasites who look to get someone into a job so they can make their buck **3.** will call you saying a **friend** of a **colleague** of their **boss** gave them your name to talk to you about some great **opportunities** that in reality are jobs you would never want, and then pump you for a name, any name, of someone who might be interested

refrigerator 1. an appliance used for storing perishable food or other items at a low temperature **2.** tiny, public cold place where employees store their leftovers, yogurt, and soy milk to put in their coffee; not unlike the **bathroom,** a location that tends to make coworkers treat each other as if they were roommates through the acts of stealing one another's food or hazelnut nondairy creamer, throwing out foul-smelling half sandwiches and stuff that is just taking up too much room, labeling items as their property, and, of course, leaving anonymous, **passive-aggressive**—or just plain old aggressive—notes scolding those who have stolen or thrown out food, or left an item in the fridge for weeks until it was a moldy, disgusting pile of sludge

reinvent the wheel 1. to do something again unnecessarily, or change something that does not need to be altered **2.** common usage: "We don't need to reinvent the wheel on this one," which means, "Let's do all we can to make sure we don't do

any work on this. Can't we take the **deck** we created for the Blimpo account and slap a new cover on it?" *See also* **repurpose.**

re-org 1. *abbr* reorganization; layoffs **2.** like its many partners in crime (**deploy,** downsize, let go, rightsize, etc.), a sanitized way of saying the company is getting rid of a lot of people, often in the name of efficiency, which really means an attempt to raise the profits and stock price **3.** following a re-org, magnanimous **managers** will understand the need for a six-minute period of mourning and adjustment, and then somberly advise those employees who remain that "the best thing **we** can do is get back to work." **4.** each shell-shocked survivor will be expected to do the work of three people, until the execs realize that they shaved a little too closely and hire back old employees (or worse, completely new, untrained people) as freelancers or **consultants. 5.** news of an impending re-org will circulate for months, causing a low-level hysteria and sense of impending doom that will drive many workers slightly insane; others staffers, in anticipation of being canned, will adopt a markedly apathetic attitude, which can be incredibly freeing and refreshing; common questions in such an atmosphere include, "What are they going to do, *fire me?*" and, "Are you/**we** fired?" **6.** the common stages of "We're going through a re-org" include shock, panic, excessive research regarding the **severance package,** job-hunting, waiting it out, fantasizing, martyrdom, apathy, acting out, and "Go ahead, make my day," in no particular order. **7.** once layoffs have begun, whether they take place over several days or weeks, an "anything goes"/Wild West atmosphere takes hold in which no work gets done, word of **hated** exec firings is dispatched with glee, and all expectations regarding appropriate workplace behavior are out the window; again, quite freeing and refreshing, and absurdist fun in the face of a disaster. *Synonyms include* downsizing, reengineering, restructuring, rightsizing, streamlining. *See also* **packaged out, merger, labor arbitrage.**

repurpose 1. to use content originally created for one format in another **2.** to not do any work but still try to make money, e.g., "We'll take the recipes from the magazine and repurpose them as Web content with some **added-value** so we can **mone-**tize our online presence." **3.** to reuse material created for one purpose for another in an effort to avoid doing work, e.g., taking a document created for one **client** and using it to present to another, less important one that may be considered **low-hanging fruit** by simply changing the name and date on it—this last part is crucial, for if you don't do it, you will be **busted;** also useful in applying for eight hundred jobs at once, but rarely effective, as most form letters are too generic to be effective and often contain errors indicating their author's lack of **attention to detail**

résumé 1. a document summarizing a person's work experience and qualifications **2.** a document that makes everything you've done seem a lot more impressive than it is due to generous embellishment of responsibilities, e.g., answering the phones and ordering **office supplies** becomes "**office** manager"; the number of staff supervised (two annoying summer **interns** become **direct reports**); skills (slapping together the invite for your summer beer blast with illegally downloaded software becomes "proficient in Photoshop and QuarkExpress");

duration of employment (an eight-month-and-two-week stint as a **temp** becomes a year on staff), and much more; in some cases an exaggeration will just be a flat-out lie, added with the confidence that no one will be able to confirm its veracity. As a result, many job candidates will furiously study their résumé the night before an **interview** in an attempt to memorize the experience of the person they are claiming to be. **3.** a document that is labored over in an attempt to find the magic layout, length, font, paper stock, and "action verbs" that will communicate that the author is a **superstar 4.** the subject of copious advice, much of it conflicting, regarding the aforementioned variables. Also the forum for ridiculous and unprofessional errors in judgment on the part of job candidates, who somehow think it's a good idea to do their résumé in the Lucida Handwriting font on pale lavender paper, submit a three-page résumé for a junior position, or smugly chronicle their world travels at the bottom of the page **5.** the document that you know you should update, you really should—but maybe you'll just watch *CSI* instead. *Also known as* **CV.**

rich people 1. individuals of extreme wealth **2.** what everyone who works ultimately wants to be; who, when met, do not deliver on the fantasy of "the rich," as they in most cases **a:** are not famous, **b:** are not fabulous or attractive, **c:** have extremely bad taste, and **d:** made their fortune manufacturing the plastic ring in your espresso-maker, or twisty-ties **3.** source of the painful dynamic in which people who are not rich try to act like they're not with, or are totally cool with hanging out with, someone who farts more money than their annual salary; leads to extended **business trips** on private yachts/expensive **dinners**/all-night binges on $350 bottles of scotch, etc., where everyone acts like they're **friends** and drinks a lot, and, unlike real **friends,** no meaningful conversation ever happens. Even the most shallow employees, if forced into the extended company of rich people, will yearn for collegiate sink bong parties, as they provided more intellectual stimulation/sincerity than hanging out with rich people. **4.** single women in the presence of rich people will speak in high tones and laugh a lot, and this will result in the offering of **gifts,** that will be refused, and then accepted after extreme insistence.

right fit, the 1. used in reference to people and current or potential positions, indicating a compatible and appropriate match **2.** most often used in a negative context, i.e., "You're just not the right fit" to provide vague, unconstructive, and irrefutable **feedback** regarding poor job performance or why you're being **fired 3.** employed as a means to reject otherwise perfectly qualified candidates (or candidates more qualified than the person doing the hiring) **4.** code for: "She threatens me." "I would not be able to intimidate and control this person." "He seems like a frat guy." "I think those shoes were from Payless." "She just bugged me." "He's too Asian," etc.

robust 1. strong, comprehensive, usually in reference to a Web site's content and functioning overall. **2.** a term ushered in by the dot-com kids in the interest of justifying their inflated salaries **3.** a fancy way of saying, "We'll be a site that actually does what our multimillion-dollar ad campaign says we're going to do," i.e., be informative and work (for example, one might say, "This Web site is really robust. It has lots of bells and whistles. It isn't full of smoke and mirrors").

ROI 1. *acronym* Return On Investment; a measure of profitability **2.** the measure of if something is worth doing at all, i.e., "That's really cool/pretty/a nice idea, but will we make any money?" **3.** the shit has hit the fan: now people have to prove that what they're doing has some value; a concept that experienced a rocket-fueled renaissance following the burst of the tech bubble. *See also* **bottom line, net-net.**

role-play 1. to act out a hypothetical scenario, most often through improvisation **2.** a common instructional technique used in training seminars and workships *that everyone **hates,*** so it's hard to understand why people still think it's a good, never mind effective, idea; individual reactions to the statement "Okay, now we're gonna try some role-play" will include groaning, rolling of the eyes, trying to make oneself as small as possible, and making a break for the **bathroom. 3.** excruciating to watch for a variety of reasons: **a:** role-play puts very uninspired and rigid people in a situation that requires a certain amount of creativity and spontaneity, and even if that means "Just talk like you would normally talk if you were having this conversation," they can't do it. Long awkward silences will be punctuated by a participant stopping to look at the facilitator and saying, "I don't know what to say," at which point the facilitator will attempt to **coach** the person, and it just gets more painful from there. **b:** frustrated former drama majors or folks who do community theater/stand-up on the side will get really into it, act as if they are auditioning for a Broadway production, and ooze self-satisfaction after their "performance," all the while dismissing with false modesty the comments from their coworkers that "That was really good." **c:** a favored role-play exercise is that of "role reversal," in which a person assumes the position of the "opposite" they are partnered with (i.e., supervisor and **direct report, boss** and **administrative assistant,** shitter and

shittee); of course, in these situations no one behaves as they actually do on a day-to-day basis, yet participants will profess to have gained "new levels of understanding" that they say they'll "take back to the **office** with them" and refer to in the future—which only serves to further underscore the fact that the exercise is a complete farce and a total waste of time.

roll out 1. *v.* to debut **2.** to introduce to the public with much fanfare and hoopla in the form of costly advertising and marketing campaigns and desperate attempts by **PR people** to get press **rollout 1.** *n.* the big moment everyone has been working toward; should it go poorly, people will get **fired. 2.** the event marking the conclusion of a **ramp up** period, during which all of the things nobody thought about, many of them painfully obvious, become crystal clear. **3.** the event that immediately precedes and necessitates a **postmortem**

S

....

sales 1. department responsible for generating revenue by selling products or services **2.** the people who ultimately pay your salary, so it's in your best interest to make sure they're happy. Without sales, you're basically out of a job. **3.** like stand-up comedians, have a very high tolerance for rejection and, unlike basically everyone else in the workforce, actually thrive on it **4.** for some inexplicable reason, many salespeople are extremely tall

secret Santa 1. a holiday season tradition in which people engage in the anonymous exchange of **gifts** of modest value **2.** a supposedly voluntary practice that really isn't, because if you decline participation, you're regarded as a party-pooper and not a true member of the **team.** Employees may claim tight finances when deferring involvement, but the real reason is "Why

on earth would I want to spend one dime on any of you people?" **3.** may involve the distribution of **gifts** in a group setting, during which everyone must open their **gifts** in front of all participants, a circumstance that creates the excruciating need to act really thrilled when you open a **gift** from someone who obviously knows nothing about you **4.** although there are rules to secret Santa, such as no **gift** should cost more than ten dollars, or all who sign up must give a **gift** (duh), someone will always receive a fifty-dollar **gift** (the **boss** being a prime candidate), and someone else will not get a **gift** at all, making that person feel like a total loser and certainly not filled with holiday cheer. The exchange of **gifts** between **friends** (orchestrated by employees trading with other coworkers to get someone they really like) will further underscore the feeling of exclusion for those not in the right **clique**

5. excellent opportunity for regifting, a reality that will lead to the appearance of lots of vanilla spun sugar bath and body gel combos with cheap plastic poofs, "gourmet" coffee assortments in flavors like mocha hazelnut and Irish cream, and the holiday gag gift du jour, à la Big Mouth Billy Bass **6.** in a nod to **diversity** and an attempt to make the tradition more secular, some companies or departments will rename it to something like "Holiday Harry" or "Jack Frost," which is not only totally stupid, but clearly smacks of "We all know it's secret Santa, but, you know, we've got to call it something else for the Jews." Despite the **brand refresh,** many employees will continue to refer to the practice as secret Santa because they can't bear to say anything as dumb as Holiday Harry.

security guard 1. a person privately employed by a company or building to monitor people entering and exiting the premises **2.** wannabe cops who take their jobs way too seriously and won't let you in the building without your **ID** even though they see you *every day;* after 9/11, these individuals became increasingly fascist and are not even open to flirtation, invocation of importance, or sweet-talking, but the guys will still give super-hot chicks a pass, because, well, they're super hot.

self-starter 1. a person who is very **proactive** in initiating their work **2.** someone who will have no supervision, guidance, or training in their job, who a **manager** can't be bothered with, or who will be brought into an irrevocably damaged situation and vainly attempt to fix it. *Please note:* watching the gung-ho people who take these jobs slowly self-destruct is great fun for crusty vets, a sport that may even inspire **office** betting pools as to how quickly the newbie will crack or quit. **3.** also code for "You are completely on your own here. We have no interest in teaching you anything. See you . . . well, see you never."

sense of urgency 1. motivation inspired by a project's extreme priority, relative to others **2.** panic **3.** visible stress that may or may not be legitimate or actual, as many employees will affect a harried demeanor to give the impression they are working hard **4.** can result in rude or abusive behavior in the name of getting something done and often contributes to increased inefficiency and mistakes borne out of an atmosphere of chaos

sensitivity training 1. company-mandated sessions designed to instruct employees on appropriate behavior in the workplace regarding **sexual harassment**, race, sexual orientation, nationality, disability, age, and religious issues **2.** this is your company spending a lot of money to finance a **PowerPoint presentation** and the **legal** department's time to say "Please, please, please don't do anything stupid that will get us sued and cost us a lot more than this presentation did—or get us bad press"; this is the thing you will complain about going to but will. The people who really need it will opt out due to a **business trip** or a packed schedule, or attend and **zone out** while they work their **BlackBerry. 3.** sessions that emphasize that *anyone* can be a victim—like the rich, white, powerful **boss,** even!—which only serves to deny the reality of sexism and power/class/prejudice **issues** in the workplace

severance package 1. compensation, in the form of a number of weeks pay, given to an employee who has been laid off by a company; may include additional assistance such as career counseling; frequently abbreviated to

"package" **2.** the holy grail, much-coveted Get Out of Jail Free card; particularly when subsidized by unemployment **benefits,** the source of countless wild fantasies involving international travel, "getting some time to think," writing novels, hanging out in pajamas at one in the afternoon, etc. **3.** for most people, always, always, always disappointing if not infuriating when they realize that the surrender of several years of their life translates to about a month of pay before they are destitute and applying for a job at Starbucks; exceptions to this include those who work in high-paying industries such as the financial sector. **4.** also source of interminable waiting games and gambles as people endlessly analyze their chances of getting laid off and weigh it against the possibility of getting one of the few positions within the company they can apply for or offering themselves up as sacrificial lambs **5.** rules change when the **CEO** is **fired.** *See also* **going in a different direction, golden parachute.**

sexual harassment 1. the execution of unwanted sexual advances or remarks of a sexual nature, particularly by a person in a position of authority **2.** supposedly, in the enlightened and newly sensitized business **culture,** verboten and an action that is met with **zero tolerance;** however, extraordinarily common; a behavior not exclusive to men—there are plenty of ass-grabbing, innuendo-dropping, perved-out women in the workplace—but for the most part, one that is executed by guys, fed by a thick-necked frat-boy mentality pervasive in the corporate **world**. Examples include an SVP of **sales** handing a female coworker a twenty-dollar bill and saying, "Thanks for last night"; a **colleague** asking a woman to "show me your tits" on a **business trip** to New Orleans during Mardi Gras; uncomfortable **dinners** punctuated by creepy touching and complaints about the wife **3.** many perpetrators of sexual harassment will attend **sensitivity training** and sit through it, confident that they do not engage in such practices, and then go back to the **office** and speak to their assistant's rack during dictation.

sexy deal 1. a business agreement with a high-profile commodity, **client,** or business **2.** descriptive phrase most frequently used in the financial sector. The problem is, the company, the deal, and the people executing it are anything but sexy.

sick day 1. a day taken off by an employee due to illness **2.** often a baldfaced lie used to squeak out a couple of extra paid days off; employed to extend a long weekend, travel to an out-of-state Wednesday night rock concert, stay in bed all day with a new romantic interest, etc. Most people would rather come to work sick and risk infecting their **colleagues** than give up an illicitly obtained and healthy day of fun. **3.** upon returning to work, employees will promptly be asked "How are you feeling?"; savvy workers will make the effort to still appear sick via taking long stretches in the bathroom or by using props such as tissues. Novices will forget they were "sick" and seem momentarily confused before lamely and unsuccessfully trying to recover from their botched lie **(busted)**. **4.** those employees who have actually been sick will have to endure massive guilt trips from their supervisor and, of course, the suspicion that they are lying. The smart employee will come back to work while still so sick, he is *sent* home. *See also* **mental health day.**

silent voicemail 1. a message that is deposited directly into a voice mailbox without the recipient's phone ringing **2.** excellent way to avoid talking to someone, especially if you're telling them something you know they don't want to hear or they are notorious for talking nonstop and holding you hostage on the phone; a cool trick, advanced corporate ninja knowledge

skill set 1. the different strengths and abilities of an employee **2.** what someone is good at, which doesn't necessarily mean she is the best at it, just that she can do it better than other things she can't do at all; a common point of discussion in **performance reviews**

sleeping your way to the top 1. having sex with people as a way of advancing one's career **2.** so Hollywood! So retro! Do people really do this anymore in our current environment of **sensitivity, meritocracy,** and **diversity?** Well, um, yes. What do you think "hold my calls," **closed-door meetings,** and those exec couches are for? *See also* **trade convention, business trip. 3.** refreshing, twenty-first-century development: men sometimes need to sleep their way to the top.

small talk 1. informal conversation between acquaintances **2.** extraordinarily painful exchanges about nothing with people you don't know and have nothing in common with; topics frequently include the weather, the most popular show on TV at the time, what you will do/did during a holiday break or weekend, **kids, weddings,** the one thing that you've ever talked about with the person— which also happens to be the thing you talked about the last time you saw him, and is the only thing you will ever talk to him about again **3.** conversations initiated to pass the time as **meeting** attendees arrive or the elevator reaches a floor; will end abruptly even if someone is in the middle of answering a question or has just asked one, universal sign that no one was listening to anyone or cared what they were talking about in the first place

SME 1. *acronym* Subject Matter Expert **2.** bloated term for someone who knows something about something. In other words, pretty much anyone at one time or another

smokers 1. people who smoke **2.** a literally dying breed, people who step out of the **office** every once in a while to smoke a cigarette, who have deep internal shame and may go to great lengths, such as walking around the corner and hiding to not be caught in the act **3.** like-minded souls who bond through their status as societal outcasts and who may be the most up to date on **office gossip** due to the exchange of information that transpires during their smoke breaks **4.** people who are **busted** for having a cigarette by coworkers who were unaware of their habit will be met with the statement, "I didn't know you smoked," which is really a way of saying, "I didn't know you were an inferior life-form." **5.** people who in a fit of desperation to get their fix will steal away to a stairway to sneak a butt—a big no-no against company policy that is clearly ignored as evidenced by the stench of smoke in the corridor and piles of cigarette butts littering the landings

smooth hair 1. hair that is sleek and free of flyaway strands, contributing to an overall well-groomed appearance **2.** particularly applicable to women; whether achieved through good genes or expensive blowouts and beauty products, a key to advancing in a corporation—these people just go farther, accept it. **3.** contributes to an overall *Stepford Wives* vibe, common among those who have **drunk the Kool-Aid, go-getters,** and **ass-kissers**

socialize 1. to interact with others in an informal manner **2.** the act of taking an idea to senior management to see if they like it, and, if so, claiming it as one's own, e.g., "I have no opinion or **vision,** so what I'm going to do is show your idea to those higher up on the ladder and see if they are into it. If they are, I'll take credit for it. If they aren't, I'll tell you all why they said it won't work in our next **staff meeting** and reprimand you for not **thinking outside the box.**"

socially unacceptable behavior 1. actions not deemed appropriate in a public forum **2.** actions that, due to an unspoken societal contract, we all supposedly agree are not allowed. And yet . . . people pick their nose and eat it in meetings, adjust their balls while talking to you, and **fart** at will at any time. Those engaging in these actions often hold positions of power and rely heavily on this dynamic to force their junior **colleagues** to ignore the disgusting act being executed and act as if it's not happening. **3.** a true symptom of those drunk on power or totally complacent, to the point that they have forgotten that other people in the room can see what they're doing—hello!? Why, people, why? Show some class.

solution 1. an answer to a problem **2.** a widely abused, vague, generic, and slightly mysterious term used to describe *products,* of all things, particularly software **3.** so overused it has lost all meaning; calling something a solution is really just a way of further reinforcing that it has **added-value.**

speakerphone 1. an option on a phone that enables the user to both engage in and hear a phone conversation without lifting the receiver; used to facilitate **conference calls 2.** function utilized by obnoxious assholes to "exhibit" their bigman (regardless of gender) "importance," who will often call people and announce that not only are they calling, but five other people with **notebooks** at the ready are "in the room" witnessing the conversation **3.** source of the "speakerphone answer," in which the recipient of a call on the speakerphone, upon hearing that the call is regarding a matter she cares about, actually lifts the receiver and continues the conversation in a tone of concern and enthusiasm; some who are fond of employing the speakerphone will often answer it with the obnoxious and brusque salutation "Yeah." **4.** a particularly evil tool in the hands of someone who occupies a **cube,** as this bigmouth will torture **cube**mates with loud and irrelevant conversations **5.** people can become misguidedly addicted to this; sign of those who have been completely seduced by the corporate milieu are AKA those who have **drunk the Kool-Aid**

sports metaphors 1. figures of speech that reference athletic activities **2.** rote figures of speech that identify the person delivering them as someone who **drinks the Kool-Aid** and is basically a soulless corporate tool who is so lazy he can't even figure out a way to express himself without using tired, frat-boy culture metaphors to convey his thoughts, e.g., "We need to knock this one out of the park." "Julie aced the **client** presentation. It was a slam dunk." And "Tom forgot the collateral for the **booth**. We're gonna have to punt on this one." **3.** really annoying shorthand. The people who use it are paid enough to come up with a more articulate way of expressing themselves. *See also* **end run, touch base, deep bench strength.**

sports teams 1. groups of people who play an organized and competitive athletic activity together **2.** at the corporate level, joining one is a truly excellent way to **kiss ass,** show "**team** spirit," and appear as a "joiner"; if you can stand being seen by coworkers in unflattering shorts/sweats and a baggy T-shirt, go for it. Be forewarned that the requisite tan and buff guy and the skinny and hot chick will be on hand to serve as a ready comparison to all else involved. **3.** a "level playing field" (*see* **sports metaphors**), in that everyone from the **CEO** to the **mail room** guy is eligible to play and is an equal on the field—in fact, it's a chance for the **mail room** guy to humiliate/save the **CEO** if he is of greater skill. **4.** worth joining one, if only to attend the mandatory postgame beer and wings

fest, during which essential **office gossip** may be dispensed and inappropriate behavior may ensue, especially because these gatherings are grittier than the more refined "**drinks** after work" activity and people may be more inclined to let it all hang out—especially if they hit a home run or something. Many people will join for the sole purpose of attending the beer and wings gatherings. **5.** group activity that can bring out the best, and worst, in coworkers in the form of the shlubby guy from **legal** who reveals himself to be a kickass first baseman to the dude who is weirdly intense and competitive about the games and acts like he's in a professional league **6.** create the bizarre sight of opposing groups of pale/pasty/underweight/overweight/cerebrally focused people attempting to engage in athletic pursuits; will also result in **office** creatures yelling/attempting to yell in a rousing and macho manner, which just makes everyone uncomfortable

staff meeting 1. a regularly scheduled **meeting** of members of a group such as a department or **team 2.** weekly, biweekly, monthly, etc., **meetings** during which the same **issues** are discussed every time, the **boss** delivers a group ass-whipping (or possibly some individual ass-whippings to reinforce employees' feelings of fear and submission), and the possible communication of mundane housekeeping information, e.g., "Please remember we don't have Christmas Eve day off." **3.** some **managers,** in an attempt to encourage **team**-building, will force employees to share with their coworkers updates on the projects they have been working on, which degrades into an uncomfortable, rote show-and-tell session during which employees say what they think the **boss** wants to hear; a total waste of time, particularly because every employee already knows what everyone else is working on because they all talk about it when they go out for **drinks**

stealth marketing 1. a technique used to create awareness through methods that introduce people to products without overtly selling to them **2.** a sure sign of the beginning of the end, when you can't even walk down the street or get a drink at a bar without some college student posing as a caricature of a hipster asking you to take a

photo of him with a camera you've never seen/they could never afford, or talking animatedly about martinis made with clove-infused vodka **3.** something that will make you feel dirty and used if you unwittingly participate in it, and afterward read an article about in the *New York Times,* a **trade publication,** or a **blog,** the last of which may include an item written by one of those college students posing as a hipster making fun of the people they engaged while making seven dollars an hour to hang out at a tourist destination or a bar—as well as the company that hired them

step down, resign 1. to formally give up an **office** or position **2.** reserved for senior members of an organization who are actually getting forced out, **fired,** or are pissed about a corporate shakeup that made their job irrelevant or didn't promote them; outgoing execs will often cite the need to spend more time with the family at their country estate, and their desire to work on unnamed independent projects. Look for these officers to resurface working for the competition in the future, or within the organization they left, but in a different position. *Also see* **golden parachute.**

subcommittee 1. a group formed to address in more detail a topic related to a larger **issue 2.** a great way for a junior employee to make a grab at power, by either being a member of this group or, even better, chairing it; training wheels for extreme politicking with the big boys **3.** forum for small-minded, earnest, and pathetic infighting among wannabe young turks who battle for supremacy regarding **issues** that no one on a senior level cares or even knows about

Successories™ 1. company that produces motivational and inspirational **premiums** such as posters and plaques dedicated to defining words that are commonly used in a business environment **2.** bar none, the black belt **superstars** of corporate bullshit, who pair high-quality stock photos with "definitions" of words like "Excellence," "Determination," and "Challenge." Totally awesome for their ironic and kitsch value. If you work in an environment where Successories are displayed in earnest, you have entered the ninth circle of hell. (But you knew that already.)

superstar 1. a person of exceptional quality and abilities **2.** often used when describing the desired candidate for a job; frequently invoked in the temporary staffing industry **3.** a largely fictional concept, a Platonic ideal, a mythical corporate superhero who is a master of wildly different disciplines—like contract negotiation, designing and writing HTML code, etc.; also, let's face it, we all know who we work with, and superstar is not on the long list of words we'd use to describe any of them. Those few who truly are superstars are scary, extremely annoying automatons who are clearly driven by early childhood trauma, have no personal life whatsoever, and, from all indications, lack a soul. **4.** use in the **temp world** is particularly counterintuitive, quite rightly begging the question from applicants who are essentially looking to bring in some much-needed cash, "If I were a fucking superstar, do you think I would be doing *this?*"; equally applicable to requests from small-potato companies that run absurd help wanted ads steeped in delusion, asking, "Are you a superstar?" "Do you have a **passion** for **excellence**?" etc., i.e., "If I were a superstar, why the hell would I work for your tacky second-tier company? I'd be taking the genius test at Microsoft."

support staff 1. employees such as **administrative assistants,** secretaries, etc., who tend to daily tasks such as filing, scheduling **meetings,** and answering phones **2.** the grunts of the workforce who make the place run. Sometimes recent college grads (*read:* low pay), sometimes highly experienced professionals (lifers who are well compensated for their discretion, skill, and loyalty). Without them, **lunch** reservations would not get made, phones would go unanswered, staplers would not get filled, and insincere small talk would go unspoken. **3.** know all the dirty secrets and best **gossip;** could very well run the company, and have a dartboard of the **boss's** face in their den

swamped 1. to be overwhelmed with work **2.** when someone claims to be swamped, they are actually saying, "I don't want to do that, and I'm not doing that." **3.** when someone else says, "I know you're swamped," this will be followed by a "but . . . ," which will be followed by a request, which means, "I'm not

swamped, but I really don't want to do this. Either you or someone who works for you will"; commonly employed by the **boss,** who will see this as **delegating,** leave for the night, and tell you to **"Go home!"** or **"Have a good night"** as they walk out the door

synergy 1. interaction of two or more forces that produces a combined effect greater than the sum of the individual forces; usually refers to the cooperative and beneficial interaction of parts of a merged corporation **2.** this is one that many people can't define, exactly, but they know how to use it in a sentence, and it sounds really sexy and convincing, especially when advocating a **merger,** partnership, or acquisition; people who talk of and **advocate** synergy frequently seem possessed and, should you look deep into their eyes, you'll notice they have unnaturally enlarged pupils. **3.** foundation of the multimedia corporation that produces content or product, markets it, advertises it, and distributes it all under different trusted **brand** names, and hopes no one will notice they are carefully masterminding everything the public sees and are taking over the world **4.** a word that is really pathetic when a random middle **manager** uses it in a **budget presentation,** because he doesn't know what it means, and he's about to be laid off as a result of a **merger** executed with the **goal** of creating maximum synergy

T

....

T&E 1. *abbr* travel and expense; refers to a travel and expense form, which documents and categorizes the money an employee has spent in a work-related activity such as a **client dinner** or a **business trip 2.** hell. The only place where your **attention to detail** really will have a significant role in your work life, because if you don't have it, you'll spend hours trying to make the numbers on potentially dozens of crumpled and beer-stained receipts add up. Your frustration with the T&E may grow so great that you decide it's worth it to pay for everything yourself just to release yourself from the torture of the dreaded T&E. **3. managers** with staff who can pawn off doing their T&E on junior members of their **team** will do so in a red-hot minute, but won't have any idea of how to file one correctly; they will, however, reprimand the junior staffer for not expensing the manicure they received prior to the **client meeting**—now *that's* **attention to detail. 4.** opportunity for creative accounting, in which **drinks** with your ex are billed as "research," and the printing of the invites to your dad's **retirement party**—which a Fresh Air Fund **kid** attended— is detailed as "community relations"

take it to the next level 1. to elevate or increase **2.** to ratchet up; may be used in reference to intensity or performance, but often is just thrown out there for effect, leaving the "it" undefined

takeaway 1. information a person derives from a **meeting** or interaction, and the action they must take regarding it **2.** the work you need to do after a **meeting** or conversation **3.** an impression or feeling, e.g., "My takeaway from the fact that I can't get an interview in-house is that, in fact, the company's **talent** is not its greatest resource."

talent 1. a special, often creative ability **2.** according to corporate **memos,** all of the people who work for a company who are allegedly deeply valued; in reality, the people who are actually important to an organization because of what they **bring to the table** in the form of skills, knowledge, contribution to a revenue-generating center, connections, etc.—everyone else is expendable. **3.** a term used to refer to those of some notoriety due to actual demonstrated talent (i.e., the ability to do something well that many of us cannot do at all) or, more likely, for just being famous, or slightly famous, or famous enough—even though they're kind of fat and bloated and have been doing infomercials in L.A. to pay the rent—to warrant the company spending money on because it's thought the investment can generate profits, i.e., "I had such a crush on him in 1981—buying his cereal makes sense!" **4.** regardless of the previously mentioned strata, frequently fussy, difficult, huge prima donnas who will be fawned over and catered to by

PR people who only serve to enable the false sense of superiority and **entitlement** of the talent, which will lead to the celeb making absurd and unjustifiable demands; this can be comforted only by the **justice** that in less than a year, no one will answer the talent's **manager's** phone calls. **5.** should you, in the course of your job, encounter a person of talent who is actually normal, kind, and decent, you will defend their reputation to the death, as they make you think there is still hope for humanity.

team 1. a group of people working together in a complementary and supportive manner to provide optimal results **2.** Orwellian term for department **3.** a condescending illusion invoked by **managers** who ignore the fact that their staff engages in constant self-interest, one-upmanship, sabotage, and general laziness when it comes to their coworkers, due to ambition or just plain apathy, and, in fact, are too busy just trying to do or keep their jobs—and, of course, the fact that some people on the "team" **hate** each other or don't give a shit **4.** the group that **managers pass the buck** to when results are less than stellar, when in fact they themselves have impeded the work of their employees via **micromanaging, managing up,** or exhibiting a general lack of **leadership** and communication

team player 1. valued employee who can be relied upon and makes significant contributions to a group **2.** an employee who will take a hit for the **boss,** is willing to sacrifice virtually all quality of life in service of his job, turns a blind eye to unethical or illegal behavior executed by higher-ups, and likely engages in copious amounts of **kissing ass**

tech bully 1. employee responsible for technical support of equipment or software such as computers, networks, servers, **BlackBerrys,** etc., hired ostensibly to help staffers of other disciplines and **skill sets 2.** an employee, most often male, responsible for technical support of equipment or software such as computers who in actuality helps you very little, thinly veils his or her contempt for your ignorance in an area you were not hired to be proficient in, and frequently commandeers your workstation for brief periods of time only to disappear without a trace after crippling your computer **3.** if male, macho discussion of hard drive size and capabilities or about an emerging technology learned of at **trade conventions** like PC and/or Mac Expo serves as smoke screen for their total lack of a romantic life **4.** when asked difficult questions in **meeting** settings or faced with tasks that may require hard work, will often revert to tech speak in an effort to confuse and intimidate fellow employees and ultimately evade giving a straight answer

telecommuting 1. to work from a remote location through the use of telephone, fax, and **e-mail 2.** similar to **working from home**, except that it is possible to telecommute from the beach or your chalet in the Swiss Alps, or a remarkably soothing estate in Chappaqua

temp 1. temporary employee; a person brought in on a short-term basis to perform a job **2.** the true anthropologists of the workplace, who drop into an **office** for a few days or weeks, are horrified by what they see, and thank God they haven't given up their dream of being an actor, artist, or freelance whatever **3.** may sit at a desk and do literally nothing all day, calling into question why they're there; may sit at a desk and, having nothing to do, receive nasty looks from the people who are supposed to be giving them work as they read a book or surf the Web in an effort to fend off **boredom 4.** if filling in for an assistant on extended leave, will be expected to know every idiosyncratic whim of the people they are working for despite completely incoherent notes left by the employee they are replacing and unpredictable mood swings from the **boss 5.** the lowest person on the totem pole at work, bar none. No one will say "hello" to this person or know his name, unless they have to because he becomes permanent, e.g., "He's just that temp guy, you know the one, always wearing that orange T-shirt." "Oh, yeah, I think I know who you're talking about. . . ." **6.** occasional and briefly exciting source of a hot new person on the floor that results in weird mating or flirting rituals and fierce, bitter competition between the single people and those open to adultery on the floor

Thank God it's Friday 1. expression spoken to coworkers on the final day of the workweek **2.** a mind-numbingly obvious statement from the catalog of **office small talk** spoken to those

you really have nothing to say to; usually answered with a "Right?" or "Tell me about it!" and a good-natured titter **3.** may be offered through a hung over haze, as the true/more honest/accurate hailing-of-the-end-of-the-workweek is "Thank God it's Thursday, because that means I can go out and get loaded tonight and basically coast to the weekend"

Thanks 1. an expression of gratitude **2.** spoken or written by senior staffers when they are giving a order; not really a phrase of appreciation for a favor or job done, but a way of punctuating a demand and ending a discussion that never was a discussion in the first place. **3.** a subtle bitch-slap in the form of a pleasantry, e.g., "If you are going to be away from your desk for more than fifteen minutes, you need to let me know. Thanks," "That report needs to be completed by Monday first thing. Thanks," **"Going forward,** I need you to make the filing of my personal bills your top priority. Thanks."

thanks in advance for your help 1. an expression of appreciation for an act not yet done **2.** the closing remarks on an **e-mail** telling you to do something when you have no choice in the matter: "Oh, you're doing it. Just tell me when it's done." *See also* **passive-aggressive.**

therapy 1. treatment of mental illness or disability **2.** if you're not in it now, you will be soon; don't bother with **EAP;** go for the good stuff and check out your **benefits** for the whole hog once-a-week deal—you'll need it.

think outside the box 1. to disregard existing ideas, policies, **solutions,** etc., when addressing a **challenge,** with the aim of producing inventive and groundbreaking answers or results **2.** phrase invoked to an exhausted, overworked, and oppressed staff to generate creative answers to **issues** in an environment that discourages and punishes individual problem-solving and creative thought **3.** usually brought up when there is zero funding in a **budget** to finance any ideas, i.e., "Figure out how to do this for no money." **4.** a directive that asks employees to attempt to change the formidable, immutable, and sluggish foe of existing corporate policies; a phrase often spoken in the company of **no idea is a bad idea 5.** ironically, a trite and

clichéd phrase used to encourage employees to have ideas that are not trite and clichéd

thirty-thousand-foot view 1. a high-level or macro view **2.** a perspective that does not account for crucial details and affords people the luxury of speaking in sweeping generalities; adopting this **tone** in a presentation is an effective way to avoid talking about a plan or project's potential pitfalls. *See also* **big picture.**

this will be reflected in your bonus 1. a statement from a **manager** indicating that an employee's year-end **bonus** will be positively influenced by their high performance on an individual project at another point in the fiscal year **2.** frequently spoken on Wall Street, where many employees hold out for their year-end **bonus;** the corporate equivalent of a dangling carrot. Unfortunately, all too easy to say (talk is cheap), and there is no real accountability for a statement made in casual conversation seven months previously (the "accountability" is the employee **quitting** because he is pissed). A sentiment that is so overused, it has become laughable and fodder for jokes among employees, e.g., a coworker passes someone toilet paper in a **bathroom** stall and they are told "**Thanks.** This will be reflected in your **bonus**."

3:45 run 1. an outing that takes place at 3:45 P.M. **2.** prompted by plummeting blood sugar levels, **boredom,** or the need for a cigarette; the act of leaving your work space to buy **candy,** have a smoke, or just blow about fifteen-minutes so that by the time you get back, it's basically 4:00 P.M. and you can just coast until quitting time. *See also* **holiday halo effect.**

360 review 1. comprehensive review of an employee in which **feedback** is provided by coworkers from all levels and areas of an organization or department as well as by professional **colleagues** and **clients** outside of the company **2.** a performance evaluation tool largely applied to senior management; a complete waste of time and company resources **3.** 360 reviews are magnanimously instigated by upper management itself with the **goal** of soliciting creative **feedback** as to how they can be better **managers** ("We get to review you, it's only fair that you get to review us.");

an elaborate internal **PR** stunt used to feign an interest in what the underlings of a company have to say **4.** may be used as a technique to quell employee discontent with the reasoning that letting people spout off and vent their frustrations will be enough to soothe the savage beast of the worker bees. Often produces no results; problems that are addressed as a result of this process will be the **low-hanging fruit** (i.e., getting everyone a mouse that works, allowing people to have **plants** on their desk, or curbing the theft of items from the communal **refrigerator**) as opposed to "timelines for projects are unrealistic and set us up for failure" and "the **mission-critical** system is always crashing"; may also, unfortunately, result in the formation of an **initiative 5.** 360 reviews used as part of an overall development tool such as **coaching** or a **management training program** curiously allow supervisors to select the people who will review them, thereby almost ensuring **feedback** that is favorably skewed and entirely omits the true opportunities for growth of the person being reviewed; a farce that enables **incompetent** and abusive managers to go undetected, unscathed, and unfired for years

Timbuktu 1. application that enables computer technical staff to access your computer remotely **2.** if you still need a reason to be completely paranoid and believe in Big Brother, this is it, kid. **3.** an application that is most frequently used to help you solve a computer problem without an actual person coming to your workstation, that results in some guy on the phone being able to move a cursor around your desktop while you watch; feels really freaky and like you're being sexually violated. Source of potential embarrassment/**busting** if you've been shopping for lingerie or dating online, and left a browser window open, been working on your résumé, etc.

time frame 1. the amount of time allotted to complete a task **2.** the amount of time you can put off doing a task, minus a day or so, e.g., "Their time frame demands delivery on Friday, so I figure I'll start cracking Thursday after lunch."

time management 1. the idea of structuring one's workday to efficiently handle multiple and varied tasks with the **goal** of giving maximum output and quality **2.** what you will be told by your **manager** you have problems with if you are completely overworked and could not complete all of your tasks even if you never left the **office** or had a twin futon in your **cube;** used to justify the inhumane workload you bear and, adding insult to injury, fuel the impression that you are disorganized and **incompetent;** always on a junior employee's **goals** and/or **performance review,** and never fulfilled to maximum expectations. As there is always more work to do, especially **busywork,** which, of course, is never-ending **3.** strategies for improving time management are often dispatched from fantasyland and, if employed, could result in disciplinary action, e.g., "Set aside a block of time during which you don't answer phone or respond to **e-mails.**" **4.** does not apply to management, who "manage *their* time" by taking two-hour **lunches,** engaging in personal phone calls, and interrupting your workday/netsurfing time by popping in your **office** to make sure you are doing **busywork**

time sensitive 1. the state of a project being linked to a future event **2.** what your **manager**

162

says to communicate that something must be treated with a **sense of urgency,** or, "Oh shit. I forgot about this, but I'm not going to admit it to you. I'll just act like it just came across my desk," i.e., we're out of time

time stamp 1. an embedded electronic indicator of when a form of communication, such as an **e-mail** or phone message, was executed **2.** great way to let your **boss** or coworkers know you were in the office at 7:00 A.M. or worked until midnight; common tactic employed by martyrs and **ass-kissers 3.** also great way for you to be **busted** for coming in late, etc., so keep in mind that it works both ways

title 1. rank and position of a person in an organization **2.** often vague description of what a person does, e.g., Business Productivity Adviser, Enterprise Solutions; slightly confusing in that there can be twenty executive vice presidents, seventeen senior vice presidents, etc., the more prestigious a person's title, the more esoteric and unquantifiable their job description will be and the faster their calls will be returned **3.** what many **colleagues** will inquire in the first few minutes of a conversation, to determine if they should listen

to anything you have to say/**kiss your ass 4.** some companies will insist on referring to employees with a title that sounds a lot better than "slave who makes minimum wage," such as "associates" or "cast members," or invent titles in an effort to exoticize a position, e.g., referring to members of a **PR** firm as "storytellers." *See also* **card.**

tone 1. mood that affects others **2.** what executives who are so self-delusional that they think people are looking to them for cues or guidance see as their job to "set"; dictated by their **boss,** otherwise they wouldn't care; attached to high-flying ideals such as "respect," "tolerance," "accountability," and "collaboration" that executives communicate through mandatory workshops and speeches delivered in the **management tone 3.** may be the direct result of an **initiative**

toner 1. a powdered ink used in a printer to create a document **2.** something a printer needs to make it work, and when it's not there it's really a bitch, as it requires calling someone who may even be outside of the building to replace it, or it's really expensive or something— what's the deal with toner? Isn't it **mission critical**? And why aren't there bushels of it lying around?

top-heavy 1. organizational staff ratio that strongly favors management positions to junior employees and people in **support staff** positions **2.** a situation in which you have eight people doing nothing, looking at the **big picture** while simultaneously **micromanaging** and making more money (AKA justifying their salaries) than the two people who report to them; lots of people trying to look important, few people to actually do the work for the entire department

top of mind 1. in the forefront of one's thinking, or regarded as a priority **2.** a catchy phrase born for the sole purpose of using it to indicate **commitment**, i.e., "We will definitely keep this top of mind." "I'd like you to keep this top of mind."; total lip service

total compensation 1. overall amount an employee is paid, as determined by an aggregate of factors such as base salary, **benefits,** and possible **bonus 2.** a term used as an attempt to distract employees from the fact that they are underpaid

touch 1. to make physical contact with, particularly with hands or fingers **2.** to affect the outcome of or have input on something, frequently when it is not required but instead for the sole purpose of exerting one's power and **leadership** position; executives, particularly **micromanagers,** will often demand that they "touch" (although they don't call it that) a project in an attempt to put junior staffers in their place (i.e., remind people who is **boss**) or to ensure their involvement so they can take credit for something if it is a success. **3.** something the more sensitive or disingenuously earnest soldiers of the workplace such as **human resources** employees and development staffers like to do in an effort to communicate compassion; for some workers this will elicit a flood of tears, for others it will make them recoil and think very loudly, "Please stop touching me. Now. Please-stoptouchingmenow." **4.** the seed of **sexual harassment** suits

touch base 1. to inquire about a matter previously discussed **2.** a widely abused **sports metaphor** that is in fact so overused that many (*read:* most) people are not even aware that they are referring to something that happens during an athletic activity **3.** to call someone up regarding a matter you've had little communication about since you last discussed it; an act that indicates "Okay, you know that thing we talked about two months ago that you—and truthfully I—didn't think would go anywhere? My **boss** is asking me about it now, so we need to do something about it." **4.** **passive-aggressive** way of saying, "I asked you to do this two weeks ago and it's been **radio silence** since then. Are you doing this? Are you **avoiding** me? Don't make me **cc** my **boss**."

town hall 1. a large company **meeting** convened to present the organization's current achievements and future plans, communicate or reinforce **initiatives;** frequently involves a Q&A session during which employees can directly pose questions to leaders **2.** elaborate, well-orchestrated dog and pony show produced to boost company **morale** and say that everything's just great; in reality, the antithesis of a true town hall, as nothing is really open to debate or discussion. Q&A session is just an opportunity for senior exec to spit back scripted answers to any possible **issue** the **corporate**

communications team has thought might be brought up, particularly on controversial **issues;** also the one chance that the exec may be exposed as having no idea what the day to day is like at the company, when an employee asks about an **issue** that everyone in the audience knows about and the exec is stumped, after which he/she will say, "We'll look into that." *May also be known as an* all-hands **meeting** or **team meeting**

trade convention 1. a formalized industry gathering bringing together representatives from all business-related companies, including suppliers, distributors, contract workers **2.** an industry-specific orgy frequently located (for bigwigs) in cities like San Francisco and Paris and (for peons) St. Louis, Anaheim, or some random place in Texas or Florida. Notable for having lots and lots of free booze, out-of-town hookups, and the palpable presence of schmooze. Features extremely long and boring days manning the company **booth**, twelve-dollar dry ham sandwiches, an obscene amount of useless, logo-emblazoned free crap like magnets, pens, and buttons, and job-related sessions your **boss** made you sign up for.

Will require spending a lot of time in close quarters with co-workers you don't like (or worse, the **boss**), getting up at the crack of dawn, and completing a **T&E** form when it's all over **3. benefits** include the opportunity to log some frequent flier miles, the chance to get some trade show love, and the free alcohol; these last two tend to go hand in hand.

trade publication 1. a periodical dedicated to reporting the news of an industry **2.** most often, really ugly magazines that cost $350 a year to subscribe to and enable workaholics with a never-ending supply of the minutiae of industry developments; feature really bad photos of people in the Personnel column (who's moving/leaving/being hired), made-up language known only to those in the "business," useless job listings, and full-length articles on the most boring topics imaginable ("Breakthroughs in UV Coating";

"Fixed Rate Mortgage Marketing Yields Big Gains"; "Online Travel Booking: The Wave of the Future"; "Pop-ups: Not Just for Kids Anymore") **3.** even the least glamorous industry has its own magazine: *Supermarket Weekly, Trucking Monthly, Jeweler's Digest, Sanitation News,* etc. **4.** may be staffed by editors and writers who joined to get their foot in the door, who are now **pigeon-holed**, ghettoized, and really sad and/or bitter

twenty-four seven 1. literally, twenty-four hours a day, seven days a week **2.** extremist, trite, unrealistic language used to communicate **commitment,** ripped off from hip-hop culture, which dispensed with it at least fifteen years ago **3.** whatever; whoever promises this is clearly lying, as most people are trying to work as few hours and days of the week as possible, and even customer service lines take a break.

U

■■■■■■■■■■■■■■■■■■■■■■■■■

UGC 1. *acronym* User-Generated Content **2.** less work for people who work on a Web site; awesome! **3.** shortcut to a big payday: "I have a great idea for a site. It's an engine that doesn't do anything, but allows people to do something they couldn't do without it—like eBay or Blogger. So I don't have to come up with any content, or anything for that matter. I'll build it, they will come, and I'll get rich. Sweet."

Unemployment 1. unemployment compensation; federal funds supplied to those who have lost a job **2.** if you've never gotten this, you are under the false impression that if you lost your job it wouldn't be so bad because you'd have free money coming in, and you could see a few less movies and sell stuff on eBay to make up the difference; if you have, you really try to avoid losing your job. *Please note:* you get this if you're laid off, but not if you quit, and sometimes when you're fired. **3.** even though it's a paltry sum, you should never feel shame about receiving this: every single paycheck from the time you began working has contributed to this government program. You deserve it, and hell, you literally paid for it.

unprofessional 1. not in accordance with behavior expected from employees working in an environment or field **2.** a phrase open to wild interpretation, that suddenly and conveniently appears at the whim of **managers**—who are unprofessional all the time—when you do something that displeases them (i.e., it's okay for them to have a freakout regarding their **office romance** and shut their **office** door for an hour, but highly unprofessional for you to do so because your mother is in the hospital; it's okay for them

167

to send a **nastygram** to someone who is a jerk, but totally out of line for you to do so; it's okay for them to waltz in at 10:45 A.M. but very unprofessional for you to not be on **time**) **3.** a total shocker when someone accuses you of being it, because it defies all you endure and witness on a daily basis

up is down, down is up 1. an illogical circumstance in which all rational and reasonable thought is not applicable or valid **2.** essentially, everyday life in corporate America: those who are **incompetent** are rewarded, working hard reaps no rewards, finally not giving a shit about your job gets you promoted, showing up hung over and unprepared for an **interview** gets you the job, etc. *See also* **justice.**

up to speed, get someone 1. when one employee passes on information regarding a topic to another employee, who possesses less knowledge on the subject being discussed **2.** an order that **managers** love to give

("Jim, after this **meeting,** why don't you get Charlie up to speed on the Barker account?"), and employees **hate** to hear, as they must go through the motions of heading back to an **office** or **cube** and have a pointless, thirty-second conversation about something the person who needs to be brought up to speed on is already familiar with.

upbeat person 1. an individual who is consistently cheerful **2.** a coworker or **colleague** who may at first seem like a breath of fresh air due to their ever-ready smile and positive demeanor, who grow to become extremely annoying and come off as increasingly insincere and shallow with every encounter, as you cannot trust someone who seems happy all the time **3.** often **administrative assistants** and secretaries and **support staff,** who despite having demanding, **difficult people** as supervisors, will never reveal the chaos they shield—God bless them

V

vet 1. to investigate or research fully 2. to stall for time or put off by saying you need to research or investigate something more thoroughly; may make you look like someone with great **attention to detail,** but really you'll blow it off until you have to go to a **meeting** discussing it, at which point you will take the thing you had to vet out, look it over for ten minutes, and head to the **meeting**

viral marketing 1. a technique used to create awareness or use of a product that is rooted in, and fueled by, consumers distributing the product or information on their own to other potential customers 2. a strategy made famous by Hotmail, which embedded a link at the bottom of every Hotmail **e-mail** message enabling recipients of those **e-mails** to sign up for a free **e-mail** account and made viral marketing the greatest thing since sliced bread; many companies have tried to replicate this strategy and failed, because they're trying to get people to pass on something not as useful as a free **e-mail** account. 3. could not exist without the **Internet,** and the massive amounts of crap that fly around it every day, which some people, unbelievably, still read

virtual team 1. a group of people who are not in the same place, but work together on a project through tools such as **e-mail**, voicemail, and common servers 2. a term of obfuscation, often used with **clients** to describe the group of employees that has been cobbled together to work on a project, one that is not even worth the expense of getting all of the people working on it in the same place—a circumstance that would considerably improve the quality of the work done

vision 1. a powerful and fixed idea that one has or creates regarding future development **2.** a really intense word that is employed by senior management such as the **CEO,** that imbues an almost magical quality to what the hell everyone at a company is doing and why they're doing it. Like, they're Merlin or some shit. **3.** the one source of legitimate pity for a muckety-muck like the **CEO,** because, by virtue of their post, they kind of *have* to have one, and really, if you had to come up with a "vision" for your life, you might be kind of hard-pressed. "Vision?" Who are you, Yanni?

W

wake-up call 1. a telephone call made with the purpose of interrupting the sleep of a hotel guest **2.** saving grace for the overworked and hung over who must make a **meeting,** flight, or be on the **trade convention** floor at 8:00 A.M. **3.** a threat from your **boss** that indicates "You better shape up or ship out." **4.** an unforeseen development that rouses everyone from their collective coma or state of denial, e.g., a competitor's earnings reflect they've taken a huge part of your market share; eight people in a single department give notice in a three-week period; the number of **sexual harassment** and discrimination lawsuits skyrockets. May result in an **initiative, management training** programs, the hiring of a **consultant,** people getting **fired,** etc.

watercooler games 1. discussions among coworkers **2.** informal conversations between staff members; subjects include **gossip,** reality TV, **weddings,** and the status of people's efforts to find another job. **3.** favorite pastime of the **office flirt,** the **office slut,** and employees afflicted with **boredom,** the last of which will be scolded by their **boss** for spending too much time socializing, even though the **boss** will not assign them any tasks other than **busywork** to fill the empty hours

we 1. *pronoun* meaning the speaker and the person or people spoken to **2.** you. As in, "We really need to make sure this doesn't happen again" or "We're gonna have to put in some long days to meet this deadline."

wear many hats 1. to fill many roles within an organization or be responsible for a wide range of tasks, all of which are often unrelated **2.** to do the job of several people without receiving the aggregate income or title of those people whom one replaces; may produce a situation in which you manage a database and supervise junior staffers, but also answer the phones, water the **plants,** and sell subsidiary rights, which you have NO idea how to do **3.** can be the product of people quitting and no one being rehired to replace them, or getting a job at a start-up, where you're led to believe that wearing many hats will get you on the fast track to being a VP, but it really means you're doing three people's jobs and waiting for the company to turn a profit, which will happen long after you've gotten fed up and left

wedding 1. a ceremony uniting two people in marriage **2.** like the weather, something that is discussed ad nauseam if a woman in the office is getting married, a real disservice to all of womankind, especially those who have something to talk about other than the search for a dress, the color of their bridesmaid's dresses, whether they're hiring a DJ or a band, and the selection of flowers, photographers, and a cake. Cause of otherwise tolerable women turning into self-absorbed freaks who

act like they're planning the most important event of all time (which admittedly, for them, it might be, but they have no perspective on the fact that this is not the case for everyone else). It all starts with the unveiling of the engagement ring to much ooh-ing and aah-ing (and catty behind-the-scenes talk about the size of the rock, be it meager or offensively large) and just goes downhill from there for about a year. But even after that, photos of the event will still need to be looked at. **3.** extremely annoying to single people, whether they want to get married or not, but particularly if they do **4.** rite of passage that inducts one into the married people **clique;** an entrée into the pregnant women or people-with-**kids** clique

weird person 1. an odd individual **2.** the really strange employee, who may or may not be a coworker, who always stops by your **office** to chat, wants to do **lunch,** and seems to want something from you but you can't really figure out what it is; never really has much to say, just kind of hangs out. May have a bizarre speech pattern, slightly crazed look in his eyes, and seem like he's on some sort of mood-stabilizing medication

We're not curing cancer 1. an expression used to remind people of the relative, and implied lesser importance, of the work at hand **2.** spoken by someone who thinks they're totally awesome to be the person who can step back and offer a little perspective; the only proper response to them is "No shit." **3.** can be useful when working on projects that everyone is taking too seriously as a way of saying "That's it. I don't care anymore and neither should you," in which case it is a relief to hear, but only **managers** can really get away with this **4.** popular in the television industry and entertainment business overall, where the environment of high stakes, tight deadlines, megamaniacal personalities, and inflated egos lead many to behave as if they *are* curing cancer **5.** PS: *no one* is standing around the workplace saying they're curing cancer, not even the folks at Memorial Sloan-Kettering. *See also* **It's not brain surgery/rocket science.**

Where are you staying? 1. an inquiry regarding the hotel where a person is residing while on a **business trip 2.** a status thing; way of separating the minor and major players attending an event before one even gets there, i.e., "the Best Western" versus some Ian Schrager confection

whiteboard 1. large white board that can be written on and reused through the use of "dry-erase" technology and markers created for use with the board **2.** large white board present in many **conference** rooms and often used for **brainstorming** sessions, that is there more for the purpose of the person using it to publicly write things down than for the helpful display of information; a canvas for a chaotic display of information scrawled in illegible handwriting. Whiteboards outnumber the special markers manufactured to be used with them by about ten to one; at some point, in the absence of an erasable marker, someone will just use a Sharpie on the whiteboard, necessitating its replacement. **3.** most annoying use of this word is in the form of a verb, as in "Let's whiteboard this out," which is another way of saying, "Let's talk about this while writing our ideas down on a whiteboard as we do it," an activity that in and of itself is annoying; those who say this frequently **drink the Kool-Aid.**

Who called this meeting?/ Who's running this meeting? 1. an inquiry made to determine who has convened a group/ who is directing the proceedings of the gathering **2.** a hallmark of the inefficiencies of corporate **meetings 3.** if you hear either of these phrases, you should get ready to turn right around and head back to your **office,** as there's a good chance the person who called the **meeting/**is supposed to run it is not there—with any luck, you will have traveled across town to attend the gathering, which means you get more free time away from the **office** doing nothing (do not, however, tell your **boss** that the **meeting** was canceled). Overall, an experience similar to when a college professor does not show up for class. Ironically, the person who called/was supposed to run the meeting most likely lobbied really hard to get everyone together, which is why no one else can/will run the meeting because, while they were prepared to bullshit about the topic at hand, they are in no way equipped to discuss the matter intelligently.

win-win 1. a situation that is beneficial to all parties involved **2.** a situation that sounds too good to be true and therefore likely is; if someone is telling you that something is a win-win situation, it's probably a "win" for them and a little bit less of a "win" for you, perhaps even a "lose."

women who behave like men 1. females who adopt the behavior of male **colleagues 2.** in mild cases: women who, in an attempt to join a male-dominated inner circle, develop a previously nonexistent interest in sports, smoke the occasional cigar, and pepper their speech with mild profanity and **sports metaphors**. In more severe cases: women who defy company policy by smoking cigars in their office, loudly claim that they have the biggest dick in the room, ask guys "How's it hangin'?" and *organize* frequent outings to strip clubs where they do a body shot of tequila off a chick's stomach

work friend 1. a companion garnered through mutual employment at an organization **2.** a nice enough person who is good to pass the time, **gossip,** bitch, and have **lunch** with, but whom you would probably never meet or hang out with in other circumstances; should a person involved in the relationship leave the company, the relationship has a high likelihood of crumbling, as in reality, besides the topic of work and constant geographic proximity, the participants have little in common. **3.** may result in the rude awakening that the person you shared more with than your significant other on a daily basis is suddenly not part of your life in any way, kind of like how you made a best friend at summer camp and then never talked to them again

work/life balance 1. a concept promoting a healthy ratio of time spent on the job and away from it, with the **goal** of creating a more content and productive workforce; often cited as an aspect of a company that attracts and retains top **talent** and contributes to a company's status as an "employer of choice." A component of work/life balance may take the form of company-sponsored workshops and classes in nonprofessional areas. **2.** an idea, like many, that is talked about but blatantly ignored, especially in times when it is desperately needed, i.e., you have worked until 2:30 in the morning for several nights straight and are expected to be in

at 9:00 A.M. every morning, even after a project has been completed (and for junior staffers, comp time is out of the question); your dentist appointment goes long and you return to the **office** late, only to be reprimanded by your **boss;** your grandfather dies, requiring you to take a day off on short **notice** and are met with scowling **disappointment** and heavy **guilt** trips from your supervisor—all of which and more may surface during your **performance review.** However, a company's **commitment** to promoting work/life balance will offer employees access to two-hour on-site seminars on such topics as yoga, feng shui, self-determination, dream analysis, pet adoption, etc. **3.** source of deep irony in that, of course, you can partake of work/life activities or classes only if your workload is under control, and you are so overwhelmed by your responsibilities that you have absolutely no time to do anything that's not work-related. If you do attempt to take one of these classes, your manager will ask you, "How is it that you have time to do this?" and give you **busywork** to ensure you never leave your desk.

working from home 1. performing all of the duties of your job from your residence, via the use of **e-mail,** faxes, telephone calls, and a personal computer **2.** Let's get real. Hello. No one works from home. It's home—we don't work there; we work at work. **3.** waking up at the start of the workday, checking your messages, and barring an emergency, going back to bed. Watching *Animal Planet,* picking up dry cleaning, maybe taking a shower. Checking your messages, and barring a crisis, going shopping/to the movies, calling your mother. Leaving a voice message/returning an **e-mail** to serve as proof that you were working from home. Clean bathroom. Pick up **kid** from school/get baked depending on life circumstance **4.** a privilege reserved for upper management, attributed to and rationalized by their more abstract and higher **skill set** as well as their implicit superior moral compass because they make more money/went to a better school than you/are more valuable to the company than junior staffers, who by the very nature of their jobs (i.e., answering the phone) could never work from home and couldn't be trusted to do so anyway, because they'd sleep in, go to the movies, pick up their dry cleaning, etc. **5.** still way more efficient than working in the **office**

world 1. a particular business environment such as an area, industry, department, or organization; "The challenges you face in your *world* are different from the ones in ours." **2.** a really annoying way of referring to any of these that lends an air of legitimacy, respect, or exoticism to it, i.e., "I find the whole *world* of paper supply very **compelling**." **3.** implies a completely different place and culture across a great divide, like a foreign land where purple people ride jetpacks around snagging gumdrops off of the tasty trees **4.** some hyperbolic people may extend this to "universe"

Z

zero tolerance 1. a negative and immutable position regarding undesirable behavior 2. big scary phrase companies use to describe their lack of acceptance of certain behaviors such as **sexual harassment** or discrimination, or anything else covered in **sensitivity training,** to let everyone know they're really serious about it; implies that there are some lesser no-no's that they have kinda-sorta tolerance for 3. logically and widely understood to mean "if you do this, we will **fire** you," but, depending on who you are (*read:* if you're an executive or someone who is a prominent member of a big revenue-generating center), you may find that "zero" magically upgrades to "kinda-sorta" and you can stick around, an outcome that will circulate as **gossip** and have the effect of lowering staff **morale**

Zoloft 1. an **antidepressant** 2. talk to your doctor about how this might work for you, i.e., help you manage the soul-crushing insanity of your workplace/aid you in keeping your job. *See also* **benefits, therapy.**

zone out 1. to lose concentration or become inattentive 2. an instinctive survival tactic that kicks in to preserve one's sanity; employed in such circumstances as when an extremely boring **meeting** is taking place or the **boss** is telling you how you need to have more **attention to detail** or work on your **time management** skills; will require the occasional "I totally understand" or "absolutely" to confirm engagement/consciousness

Zyban 1. another **antidepressant** that might aid you in your attempts to not go ballistic and threaten your ability to make mortgage payments. *See also* **benefits, therapy.**

Very special thanks for all the work that you do:

Barret Neville: a super man, and damn good agent, too.
Andrew Corbin: an editor whose good taste knows no
bounds.

And Jonah Kaplan, who told me I could do it before I even
had the idea.

**Thanks to those who went above
and beyond and gave 110 percent:**

Joan Biddle, Steve Borst, David Boyer, Mr. Binkler, The
Bullshit Bar Brigade (Celise Kalke, Rachel Melnyk, Felicia
Roff Tunnah, Sarah Welt, Miss Eva Fwae Yun), Michael
Collica, Kathy Landherr, Carol and Nick Love, Ed and Alaine
O'Connor, J. O'Neill, Brendan Paul, Darya Porat, Nancy and
Paul Raca, Jessica Schram, Joshua Thomas, Sharyn Wolf, and
all of you who kept me sane while I was in the throes of all
the bullshit—you know who you are.

Thanks to all who responded when I reached out, and contributed some bullshit of their own:

Joseph Agresta

Prem Akkaraju

Melissa Anelli

Pal Anuvab

Stephen Baer

David Ballard

Brock Boddie

Kristin Breuss

Kenneth Briskey

Brent Brookler

J. Bumbas

Susie Chang

Howard Cohen

James Conboy

Augie Cosentino

Shari Cummings

Lisa DeBoer

Kurt and Kim Delaney

Tim Dougherty

Catherine Ewen

Mike Flanagan

Lisa Fogel

Sanderson Frrettian

Heidi Gibson

Benjamin Goldsteen

Daniel Gooch

Erinn Hartman

Daniel Horton

Russ Hurlbut

Gabby Hyman

Jonathan Isher

Elizabeth Ives

Judy Kamilhor

Jim Karpe and everyone at
   EMBA

David Kay

Terese Kelly

Amy Keyishian

Anu Kirk

Charles Kloster

Michelle Lambert

Amy Lesch

Kevin Maher

Patti Manzone

Deborah McKeand

Sarah Melnyk

Craig Mertens

Paul Mifsud

Peter Mitchell

Angela Moore

Cheryl Murray

John Nicosia

Nicholas Oliva

James Park

Louis Parks

Greta Peterman

Larry Resick

Sherry Rhodes

Anne Sachs

John Salib

Jen Simon

Jen Smith

Joel Tunnah

Andrea Turner

George Varino

Christine Wilcox

Andrew Winston

Art Wynne III

Jennifer Zambri

And the many NYC happy
hour patrons who
probably don't remember
talking to me

Lois Beckwith is a corporate communications executive at a major media company in New York City.